The Valley of Ritualism

Hinduism and Rishikesh from a Religio-Spiritual Perspective

SAMANVAYAM - *Contextual theology series–11*

The Valley of Ritualism

Hinduism and Rishikesh from a Religio-Spiritual Perspective

Cyril Kuttiyanikkal

2021

Contents

Chapter 7

Chapter 8

Acknowledgements

This is a small introduction to Hinduism and an explanation of the Hindu rituals, ashrams, yoga centres, temples, and spirituality visible at Rishikesh. In this work I have tried to give a brief description and a short explanation of the rituals, symbols, and life of devotees, pilgrims, and monks in Rishikesh. This is intended as a guidebook for anyone who comes to Rishikesh for the first time or for anyone who wants to understand the meaning of Hinduism with its symbols and rituals. I have not included every aspect of Hinduism but only those which are visible, and which are essential in understanding what Hinduism is.

This book in fact is almost like a second edition to my earlier work *Fortress of Solitude,* but with more details and additions. Basically it is the outcome of my own exploration of life and rituals at Rishikesh. But the actual inspiration to write it as a book is the result of the enquiries from the visitors and pilgrims. The questions and queries from visitors, especially from non-Hindu background encouraged me to write this book so that they can take it with them as a guidebook and a handbook. Besides the explanatory sections, I have also included a small section introducing the framework of Hinduism in chapter 6.

This section of Hindu worldview will make it clear, the 'why' of these rituals. It is a small work; hence the reader can finish reading it in one go.

Many people have contributed to compiling this task. The photos in this book including the covers are the result of the keen observation and hard work of Prince Punnan. The title of the book was suggested by Rinto Porathukaran. Several information and explanations about the rituals were given by Swami Govindanandji. The manuscript was read and corrected by Dr. Yann Vagneux, who also provided me with much of the information of the last chapter of this book. I am also indebted to Swami Abhishek for taking me around and introducing me to the hidden lanes of Rishikesh and giving all the needed support for this venture. The discussions with Aranya Mataji also have helped in the formation of this volume. There were many others who share the credit for this work especially, Mr. Sushant Pandey, Mr. Uttam Gosh, and above all my students and staff, especially Fr. Jose Chittooparambil and late Fr. Louis Malieckal at Samanvaya Vidya Dham. I am also indebted to Rishikesh Yogis Yogashala for giving me the details of the yoga centre.

Cyril Kuttiyanikkal

Introduction

Rishikesh –An Introduction

Rishikesh is a small town nestled in the green lush of lower Himalayas of Shivalik hills, vibrating a spiritual atmosphere from sages, ashrams, and temples. The very name Rishikesh evokes a sense of reverence, awe, and otherworldliness in the Hindu devotees. The word Rishikesh comes from Hrishikesh of which the root words are hrishik (senses) + ish (master or Lord) that means the Lord of the senses which is Lord Vishnu. Thus it is a place where one tries to master the senses. The myths speak about sage Raibhya who mastered his senses by performing austerities here. In Skanda Purana this area is known as Kubjmarak since Lord Vishnu appeared under a mango tree. Sage Raibhya sat under a mango tree performing penance and tapas because of which Lord Vishnu appeared and granted a boon to the sage. The sage asked Lord Vishnu to dwell in this place for ever, which the Lord granted.

This holy city came to the attention of the Western world when the English rock band 'the Beatles' together with their team came to Rishikesh to attend the Transcendental Meditation(TM) training session at the ashram of Maharishi Mahesh Yogi, in the year 1968. Several news reporters also joined them and this small city until then hidden in the foothills of Himalayas in its natural splendour as the abode of yogis, monks and sages came to be known as the religio-spiritual centre of India. Today it is styled as the yoga capital of the world with all kinds of yoga teacher trainings or meditation centers.

However, visitors are spellbound by the spectacle of river Ganges rushing through the mountains and entering the serenity of the plains at Rishikesh. As you stroll down to the banks of the Ganges, it becomes lively with pilgrims both Indian and foreign, mingling into one stream of humanity. Several temples, ashrams, yoga and meditation teaching centers dot the banks of Ganges. Swamis, yogis, and ascetics wearing various coloured clothes and practicing penance, tourists and pilgrims attending aarti and other rituals is a site to behold the eyes of any visitor. Foreign visitors throng to Rishikesh mostly from the month of February to April to listen to the discourses of foreign gurus while Indian visitors flock the town from May to October both to listen to Indian gurus and since this city is the starting point for the pilgrimage to char dhams. Other foreign visitors come to attend the yoga teacher training courses offered in several centers in Rishikesh or to attend the international yoga festival which is held in March.

One can also learn different kinds of yoga- hatha, shahaja, classical etc., or listen to the discourses on spiritual life or Hindu scriptures, as well as learn to play musical instruments like tabla, harmonium etc. Many foreigners flock to Rishikesh seeking spiritual enlightenment from teachers and healers in the small and big ashrams scattered throughout the banks of Ganges. There are also courses on several things like reiki, ayurvedic massage and even cooking. Rishikesh also has now become popular among the Indian youths as the tourist spot with focus on rafting, bungee jumping, staying at tents and trekking.

However, Rishikesh still remains as the place where spirituality dominates. Religiosity flows through the banks of River Ganges. The whole atmosphere of Rishikesh is one of spirituality and rituality filled with sacred scenes and symbols. Although the religious rituals are visible, the meanings of those rituals are not traceable to someone who is not familiar with Hinduism. It is true that the local guides will be able to explain the rituals and the importance of each place with its history; they may not be able to give an analytical exploration of these rituals, penances, and actions. Therefore in this work I would like to present an explorative study on the life at Rishikesh with its ashrams, temples, yoga centres and pilgrimage. First, I shall focus on the descriptive aspect followed by the explorative work.

As we walk through the shores of Ganges and the streets of this small town, we come across several religious activities and rituals. Therefore first I shall start with presenting the rituals and religious activities visible at Rishikesh. I shall also be presenting the reasons why the Hindu devotees take up such rituals and penances. On the one hand, the Hindu devotees are engaged in several religious activities and rituals, on the other hand, the whole atmosphere of Rishikesh is encompassed of religious symbols and signs. Hence, in the second chapter I shall take up the important signs and symbols visible at Rishikesh and make clear and interpret them. Rishikesh is known for its ashrams and religious life. Hence the third chapter will be devoted to the presentation of the Hindu asceticism and the ashrams and the life in an ashram. Ashrams in Rishikesh are so important that the very name of the city is almost like a synonym for ashram.

Therefore, I shall present the life at each of these ashrams and shall compare it with the life in Christian monasteries so as to exhibit a clearer vision of Hinduism in the context of Rishikesh. Chapter four will give a general introduction to the important temples of Rishikesh since Rishikesh is also called a temple town. Instead of giving the list of temples, I will give the name of the ancient temples and present a description of the temple worship itself so that the reader may be familiarized with temple worship. Rishikesh has gained a name for its yoga teacher training and yoga classes. Therefore the fifth chapter will give a small description of yoga and a short introduction to some yoga centres.

This explanatory section would help us to finally move towards comprehending the framework of Hinduism. The external expressions, rituals, symbols and icons do not really convey the core of religion, but it lies beyond them. Therefore, in the sixth chapter, I shall explain the Hindu world view which will clarify the hidden meaning behind the religiosity which is visible outside. Towards the end of this chapter, I have also presented in brief an introduction to the scriptures of Hinduism. This will be followed by a small description of Hindu spirituality in chapter seven. All that is visible at Rishikesh does not speak comprehensively on Hinduism and it does not exhaust Hinduism. Hence, I shall make a brief mention of the Hinduism practiced in the rural areas just enough to say that Hinduism is not a monolithic whole but it has several trends and streams within it. And finally Rishikesh is also a place for people of all religions. The Christian presence in this area shows the inter-religious living of India. Hence the last chapter gives a small description of the presence of both the ancient Thomas Christians as well as the modern Christianity, which teaches us that for spiritual seekers religious affiliation is no barrier.

Endnote

[1] *Char dhams* are the four abodes or holy places which a Hindu long to visit at least once in his/her life time. There are two circuits of such places, the minor and major ones. The minor ones are Badrinath, Kedarnath, Gangotri and Yamunotri, which are all located in the Himalayas and a pilgrimage to these centres begin at Rishikesh. Originally completed on foot, now people use transport facilities. The major *char dhams* are located in the four corners of India, namely, Dwaraka, Rameshwaram, Puri and Badrinath.

Chapter - 1

An Introduction to the Rituals and Spiritualities at Rishikesh

Hindus generally divide their religious rituals into three categories, namely *Nitya* which means daily rituals, *Naimittika* which stands for occasional religious rituals and finally *Kamya* which means rites or rituals performed in order to achieved desired results.

The daily worship/*nitya puja* takes place at home before an altar maintained as the focus of devotion which is done in the morning. The house altar can have the family deity[1] as well as other individual deities as each person in the family including the children can have their own favourite deity. The daily worship/*puja* is performed ideally three times, but at least once in the morning.

The home altar, sometimes a room or a part of the room, is treated as a temple itself. At Rishikesh also one can see people visiting the temples for *puja* in the morning. The *puja* is performed in the morning before eating anything. One takes bath, shower or at least washes his feet and hands before entering this room/temple. The performer wearing a freshly washed cloth enters the room and prepares the statue of the deity, which is called *murti*. An idol becomes the *murti* or rather identical with the deity by the ceremony called *prana pratishta*. By this ceremony the authorized priest calls the presence of God into the image so that one can communicate with the deity and worship the god who is now present in the image[2]. The statue is ritually bathed with water, milk, or honey, dried and anointed with sandalwood paste and dressed in beautiful robe. If the *puja* is formal then every participant brings with him or her flowers, coconut and sweets, incense stick, some food or water. The *puja* consists of reciting of mantras, prayers and offerings made to the deities and sun, marking of forehead, and retrieving of *prasad* offered to the deity. During the *puja* conch shell or bell is used for achieving attention and focus of mind and for vibration. It is concluded by an *aarti* which is performed to the deity and passed on to all those present for reception. If one is in a house or a place where there is no deity installed, then one faces either north or east for the *puja*. The north direction symbolizes the spiritual progress while the east symbolizes the direction of rising sun which denotes enlightenment.

The second category is *Naimittika* which stands for occasional religious rituals which is normally performed at temples or holy places during special days or occasions. It is also performed while on a pilgrimage. Such festivals, like *kumbha mela* or occasional temple festivals at the village or pilgrim centres and pilgrimage to holy places are the backbone of Hinduism.

The third category is *Kamya* and is undertaken voluntarily. It is mostly in the form of pilgrimages to sites associated with one or the other legend. Although pilgrimage is not required as mandatory, people take it up as a penance, or to purify oneself and gain God's favour.

A pilgrimage to Rishikesh and performing several rituals come under the category of both *Naimittaka* and *Kamya*. People of all age group come to Rishikesh. Most young people visit Rishikesh not for pilgrimage but rather for religious tourism and more often just to experience water rafting and bungee jumping. However many people come for pilgrimage. A good number of pilgrims at Rishikesh are the people who are either retired or seniors who spend a rather long time in search of peace and spiritual pursuit. We shall give more details of the ritual practices further down the page.

Taking Holy Bath

According to Hindu understanding bathing is not limited to cleaning the physical body, but bathing of the mind as well. Many Hindus of higher *varna* have the ritual purification *achvan* or the water ritual called *tarpan*. One can see pilgrims and devotees standing in the water to perform these rituals.

A Sadhu performing *achmana*

Achvan (also called as *achmana*) is the ritual of purifying one's body by sipping water and touching several parts of the body while reciting mantras (see 2.4 as well). It is done on several occasions especially before performing any Hindu rituals. The simplest form consists of facing the east and taking water 3 times into the palm and sipping it three times from the base of the right thumb (called *brahma grantha*) while reciting the mantra.

Tharpan is the ritual of offering water to God, sages, deceased ancestors' souls and satisfying them. The ideal place for performing *tarpan* is the riverside. While performing the *tarpan*, one stands in the river so that the water level touches the belly button, or one should perform *tarpan* by sitting on the banks of the river. When *tarpan* is performed for God or sages, the performer faces the east and for the deceased ancestor's souls, he faces the south. (More details of *tarpan* is given below at 1.9)If the water is offered to deities then he uses the finger tips, while offering to sages is done from the base of the little finger and the third finger and to the deceased ancestor's soul it is done through the mid of the thumb and first finger. Only one handful (anjaly) of water is offered for each deity, two handful for sages and three handful for the deceased ancestor's souls.

Many important temples are by the side of a river or lake so that devotees can bathe before entering the temple[3]. There is an obsessive or rather persistent concern on the part of the high caste Hindus of being polluted from the touch of the lower castes and so they observe all possible kinds of segregation.

What one observes at Ganges in Rishikesh is the ritual bathing. Many Hindus consider life as incomplete if they cannot at least once in a lifetime, take a holy dip in the Ganges. The ritual bathing is accompanied by reciting of what is called 'the bathing mantra'. It is done by taking water into the right hand[4], then drinking/sipping it from the palm of hands and then reciting the following:

apvithra: pavitrova sarvasthaam gatopivaa, ya:

smaret pudareekaaksham sa: baahyaabhyantara shuchi:

sri harirhari: pundarikakshaaya nama: iti atmanam prokshya.

(Whether a person is pure or impure that is, a person might be in any situation or condition, he can still realize his goal.) While reciting the manta one is purifying one's inner world and wipes away all the defects from within.

On special occasions one can see crowds of Hindus climbing down the *ghats* of Ganges for the ritual holy bath. According to the Hindu tradition, such festival days are auspicious and on such days the water in the Ganges transforms itself into nectar and therefore anyone who takes the holy dip is not just washing his body and mind but this holy dip will guarantee the washing away of all his sins done in his life. That is the reason why on the mega Hindu bathing festivals called *kumbh mela*, millions of ordinary Hindus and lakhs of *naga sannyasis* and all types of sub sects rush to Ganges at Prayagraj(Allahabad), Hardwar, Nasik and Ujjain where according to legends the drops of nectar had fallen into the river. People spiritually prepare, sometimes even for 12 years for taking up this pilgrimage for what is called a *kamya snan*. This *kumbh mela* occurs once in 12 years in each of the 4 sites.

Even on a normal daily bath called *nitya snan*, the first part is washing of the body accompanied by reciting of a mantra which begins with *Om aapo hi stha mayo bhuvah* and ends with *Om apo janayatha cha naha*. (It is well-known that you, the deities of water, are the cause of great happiness. Please nourish us with the divine vision which brings glory and loveliness. Please make us worthy of imbibing the auspicious bliss even as a mother feeds her children. We approach you with eagerness for that bliss to distribute which you have taken a form and are shining. Bestow on us the boon of a next life sanctified by knowledge.) Thereafter the ritual of purifying the mind begins with sprinkling of water on the head, chest, and the feet if one is not already standing in the water. This is followed by sprinkling of water in different direction. This is done again to purify the place. It is noteworthy that taking bath every morning is a revered custom in India. Every yoga especially *hatha* yoga requires taking bath as a prerequisite. The ritual cleaning however begins with washing the head and then moving down the feet. Thus bath is not just bodily cleansing but purifying of the mind and making the person ready for spirituality for which water becomes a symbol.

Taking a holy dip at Ganges is not limited to a purification ceremony but it has a much deeper significance. River Ganges is considered as sacred and is worshipped and personified as a goddess. They consider the waters of Ganges as (amrta) life-giving and feel that bathing in the river any time preferably on certain auspicious occasions causes the forgiveness of sins and helps attain salvation. After the pilgrimage to Rishikesh (or Ganges in any place) the devotees carry the water from Ganges and preserve it (preferably in copper pots) at home. Keeping the water of Ganges at home is considered auspicious. They also believe that drinking water from the Ganges with one's last breath will take the soul to heaven. Similarly, people travel from distant places to immerse the ashes of their deceased kin in the waters of the Ganges. This immersion also is believed to send the ashes to heaven. For more details see our discussion in 1.9 on the following pages.

Moreover, in the Hindu tradition water stands for rejuvenation, prosperity, and the male-female principle. According to some, Lord Vishnu is the lord of the water and his consort Lakshmi the mistress of prosperity. Therefore bathing in a river can activate the forces of Vishnu and Lakshmi in one's life.

Visiting Temples

Visiting several temples is part of the pilgrimage to Rishikesh. In general Hindus are prone to bow before *murtis* of several deities. They accept the divinity of all and so try to visit as many temples as possible. At every statue they intercede for their needs and offer their prayers. They are eager to receive blessing from any deity. Hence one can see the pilgrims going to several temples and to several statues of the same temple.

On both sides of the Ganges at Rishikesh, several temples can be seen. Some are new while others are older. Among them the ancient ones are Shatrughna temple, Bharat Mandir and Lakshman Mandir. On the outskirts of the city also there are important temples like Nilkhant Mahadev temple and Kujapuri temple. We shall speak more about the temples and temple worship when we deal with the temples in the later part of this book. Here what is to be noted is the presence of several temples dedicated to several deities of Hinduism and the importance of visiting all these temple on the part of devotees even if they have only one particular deity as their cherished deity (ishta devta).

Regular Visits to Gurus

Having a personal guru is of utmost importance in Hinduism. According to the Hindu understanding one can attain his or her salvation only by the help of his/her guru. Hence for a spiritual journey it is essential to find a guru and to follow his instructions and guidance. Rishikesh is a place where several gurus and monks live. Therefore many pilgrims come to Rishikesh to meet their gurus on a regular basis. According to Hindu tradition, guru merits primary respect over God because guru leads the disciple to God. "Guru is one who has himself ascertained the real and who knows the real from personal experience"[5]. He is able to initiate others into the same experience and knowledge of God from his own personal God-experience[6]. According to the Hindu understanding, the most important aspect of God-realization is finding a suitable guru, because without guru one cannot achieve God-realization. Hindus believe that without a human guru they would be unable to remove the darkness of ignorance from the heart. They believe that at some stage of life they should meet a guru and that meeting is considered as indispensable[7]. They simply flock to have a single look or a gentle touch of his feet, which puts some in a state of ecstasy[8]. "Choosing a guru in India is sometimes almost the counterpart of choosing a spouse in the west, or more accurately a parent"[9].

Pilgrims who accept one or the other swamis living in the ashrams or in huts as their personal guru visit them occasionally. So pilgrimage to Rishikesh is used as an opportunity to visit them, seek their guidelines and blessings.

Participating/Performing Ganga Aarti

Ceremonial Ganga *aarti* is performed in more than one place in Rishikesh. Among them three are important which attracts many visitors and pilgrims. The one at Triveni Ghat is often called the maha *aarti*. The one at Paramarth Niketan also attracts many tourists. An interesting *aarti* is performed outside the Gurudev Kutir at Shivananda ashram as well. These daily evening rituals conducted at dusk are spiritual occasions for the devotees to pay their tribute to Ganga *ma*. The *aarti* is preceded by sacrifices, singing of bhajans and chanting of mantras. While *aarti* is done everyone stands up and joins either in the singing and clapping of hands or playing musical instruments or ringing of bells. The proper *aarti*, i.e. the waving of light is first performed by either pundits or the students who study Vedas and normally passed on to those present for them to join and to perform the *aarti* themselves. At the end everyone receives the light with their hands. It is done by hovering the hands over the flame and touching their hands to their eyes and top of the head either once or thrice. The light is thus received to the eyes since eyes are considered by entrance to the soul. It is the eyes which see the light, symbol of God himself.

Aarti at Shatrughan Ghatt

Not all the pilgrims wait for the evening common Ganga *aarti* performed at three different places. What they normally perform is the personal *aarti* at the Ganges. One can see the materials needed for *aarti*, namely flowers, food, incense, and small light with *karpoor* in a paper/leaf plate, being sold at the banks of river. The pilgrims either bring their own *aarti* plate or buy them here at the Ganges to perform the *aarti* and float it in the water.

Satsangh with Gurus

Many devotees visit their gurus living in the ashrams or in the huts and listen to the spiritual discourse called *satsangh*. There are devotees who at a regular intervals visit these gurus and listen to them and take their spiritual guidance and *pravachan* or homily. Some pilgrims come as a group accompanied by a guru or a pundit and they sit at the banks and listen to his discourse.

Gurus living in ashrams other than Rishikesh occasionally visit Rishikesh, mostly accompanied by their devotees in large number. On such visits the Gurus stay in Rishikesh and give *satsangh*. So devotees from various places come to visit him, take his blessings and listen to his *satsanghs*. If the visiting guru is famous, then the number of visitors will also be large.

Parikrama of Ganges

Parikrama means circumambulation of mostly what is sacred like *murti*, temple or something which is holy like river. It is walking around in a circle which is considered as part or form of worship. Mostly devotees take a *parikrama* around the inner most chamber of the temple deity. When you enter the temple normally you first pay homage to the deity. But you do not get out directly but take a *parikrama* of the deity, always keeping the deity on your right side. Hindus also take a *parikrama* around the *tulsi* plant, sacred fire or peepal tree or even around a pilgrimage centre.

A complete *parikrama* of river Narmada (which is in central India) is possible and so every year thousands of people walk around Narmada. Some people take it up as a severe form of ritual-penance when they walk barefooted, without carrying money or food. While undertaking *parikrama*, people try to think of only God and free one's mind of all worldly thoughts. However the *parikrama* of Ganges in its full sense is not taken up as the banks of the Ganges are not walkable. Therefore most pilgrims take short *parikrama* of the Ganges starting at any point on the side of Ganges at Rishikesh crossing both the bridges on foot and returning to the same spot.

Attending the *Satsanghs* in an Ashram

Ashrams have a schedule for giving *satsanghs*/discourse to the public. The pilgrims who visit Rishikesh attend the *satsanghs* in one or the other ashrams. If possible, many will attend the whole day's programme if not at least one session. Some devotees regularly attend the ashram for short periods while making a yearly pilgrimage to Rishikesh. Some pilgrims plan for their stay in the ashram to attend the discourse while others stay in some hotels or *dharmashalas* and attend it. There are some regular gurus who come to Rishikesh annually and give discourses. Some of the famous gurus like Mooji, Sri Sri Ravishankar, Prem Baba and so on come to Rishikesh and give their discourse to the devotees.

Being in the Holy atmosphere of *Rishis* and Sages

The very name Rishikesh evokes reverence in the hearts of Hindus. The area called *Muni ki Reti* which literally means sands of sages is considered as the area where sages (munis) used to meditate or practice other spiritual austerities. This sand of sages is full of temples, ashrams, yoga centres visited by several pilgrims, devotees, and monks. Similarly the area called Tapovan which means the forest meant for austerities is also a place where sages lived alone and performed their austerities and hard life. The very atmosphere evokes in them piety and devotion. Hence devotees long to come to this holy atmosphere and spend some time in the aura of divinity and blessings.

Offering *Pujas* and Worshiping

The word *puja* means reverence, adoration, honour, worship or homage. Some Hindus offer daily *puja* while others offer only occasionally. Performing a *puja* is not compulsory for the Hindus. However, some pilgrims and devotees perform some *pujas* in the temples of Rishikesh. The physical representation of God, be it the altar, or the statue is considered as an antenna to receive the blessings of God. They believe that God inhabits these representations. Therefore when one enters the premises of these images one is entering into the area where the divine vibrations are present. The *puja* is performed to attract the attention of the divine deity.

Generally two types of *pujas* are performed in temples by the pilgrims. One is performed to gain the blessings of God or rather for the pleasure of God called *Devpujas* while the other is performed for the sake of ancestors or to please the ancestors called *pitrupujas*. *Devpujas* are performed for gaining something or the other, like gaining good health, wealth, peace, getting married, happy married life or to conceive a child and sometimes for alleviating sufferings etc.

The *pitrupujas* are conducted by the children or nearest relatives of the diseased person. The funeral ceremony is called *antiyeshti* which is ideally conducted at Ganges. However it is not possible for people living away from Ganges to carry the dead body to Ganges for cremation. Hence it is cremated at their places and the ashes are brought to Ganges within 13 days. Normally the children (eldest male) or close relatives come to perform what is called the *pind daan* ceremony.

Hindus believe that the soul or spirit of the dead person wanders around until *pinda daan* is offered. Once *pinda daan,* which is obligatory, is offered, the dead person is raised to the status of an ancestor to whom veneration and obeisance can be paid. Only after offering the *pinda daan* the soul is released from bondage. They believe that no work can be successfully completed without the blessings of the ancestors. Their blessing is also assured by offering *pinda daan.*

Every year during the special days in the year known as *Pitri paksha*, or at every anniversary of the death, *shraddha* and *pinda daan* is performed preferably at Ganges. The reason why these *pinda daan* and ancestors *puja* is performed at the banks of Ganges is that traditionally the Hindus believe that the banks of river Ganges are blessed with purification powers. The *pinda daan* involves the offerings of rice cake (pinda), libations of water called *tarpana* and oblations through fire called *homa*. By performing the *pinda daan* and ancestors' *puja* the relatives/ children help the soul of the dead person to attain salvation. They believe that it is the love, concern and affection of the family members that keep the departed soul attached to them and thereby to the materialistic world. *Pinda daan* releases the soul from these attachments. Moreover it also wards off restless spirits that can affect the family members of the dead due to performing incomplete or wrong rituals at cremation.

There are several forms of *pitrupujas*. There is something called *Tripindi* and *Narayan bali sraddha* which are performed when someone in a family has died not naturally and and by an untimely accident. The same *puja* is also offered if *pitrupuja* could not be performed three continuous years. To attain prosperity and wealth *Sahastracharanpuja* is offered. To get rid of sickness *vinayak shanti puja* is offered.

According to Hindu understanding death is a phase in life by which the soul transits from one stage to another. During this journey they consider it necessary to receive help from the living progeny. Therefore Hinduism prescribes several ceremonies on regular intervals like daily, weekly, monthly, and annually. All these rites can be placed under the umbrella term *sraadh*. *Sraadh* is performed for the departed souls of one's paternal or maternal near and dear ones. It is performed on specific days allotted for the purpose. There are also exceptions to the rules for certain kinds of death or status of life.[10]

Tarpan means satisfying, is another ritual performed by the pilgrims. *Tarpan* is also meant to satisfy the departed soul. You can see *tarpan* being performed by those standing in the water and offering water three times after taking it in the palms joined and dropping down the grass while reciting some appropriate mantras. Besides these, there are special rituals under *sraadh* for those who met with unnatural deaths. Furthermore, the Hindus believe in the curse of ancestors called *pitra dosh*. It occurs when the children or relatives have not performed the rites required to be done. It can also happen due to unnatural death or death of several people in the family. Thus the souls of such ancestors are not at peace and have not been released from this world. Hence the anger of the ancestors can bring troubles, failures, sickness, and prolonged illness of calamites on the living. In such cases the relatives or children perform *tarpan*.

Mantra Dikskha

Another important religious ritual that is taking place, albeit hidden from the visitors' eyes is the *Mantra diksha* or initiation into mantra. A mantra is a word, name of a god or a set of words accessed intuitively by saints or gurus and given by the guru to the disciple in secret in order for him to repeat as a spiritual means for God-realization. Normally the name of *ishta devta* (favourite God) is given as mantra. The aspirant is supposed to follow the instructions given by the guru at the time of initiation.

An aspirant approaches the guru with unwavering mind and firm determination for a mantra. The aim of continuous repetition of mantra is to receive God-realization and not for any other material gain. As a condition, the aspirant must give up all his negative thoughts, attitudes, and values such as greed, anger and jealousy etc., and cultivate divine qualities such as love, service charity etc. Normally the one who takes this *diskha* must repeat it daily as he/she carries out his duties and should fast on the anniversary of the *diksha*. The initiated never reveals his *mantra* to anyone. It is believed that the constant recitation and recollection of mantra will protect a person from the impact of *maya* or illusion.

Many aspirants come to the ashrams in Rishikesh for getting initiated to *mantra japa*. Gurus initiate them to the mantra and the initiated spend a couple of days in the ashram solely reciting the *mantra* alone. Such devotees are not normally seen outside wandering. But they are serious seekers of God-realization. They take spiritual life seriously and mostly return to the ashram or guru year after year for his blessings and continued guidance. The number of people seeking this *mantra diksha* in Rishikesh ashrams is on the increase.

Visiting Astrologers

There is a deep belief in Hinduism that human life is influenced by the movements of the planets and astrology is of vital importance in determining an auspicious time, even down to the correct hour to undertake major events and rituals[11]. There are several Vedic astrologers and palm readers in Rishikesh. Astrology is particularly important in determining the degree of auspiciousness of important events in life. They give advice/ solution to people's problems concerning career, job, marriage, investment etc. People approach them for horoscope matching or horoscope compatibility for marriage. They have solutions for all kinds of problems faced by the people. Some of these astrologers also run online astrology courses as well. There are some centres which provide palmistry course, astrology course, reiki course etc. People approach these masters on various issues like education, career, professional growth, love life, marriage, childbirth, financial condition, property, and health issues. They make astronomical and astrological calculations and suggest ways and means.

Pilgrimage

All the above-mentioned rituals are taken up in Rishikesh by the devotees as part of their pilgrimage. Since ancient times, pilgrimage was considered as an integral part of Hinduism. Most of the pilgrim centres in India are in remote areas and travelling to those difficult areas were considered as mark of one's devotion and commitment to religion. With the advancement of means of transport and communication, pilgrimages have become more popular. Every pilgrimage has the aspect of *yatra* (travelling), *darsana* (vision of the deity) and *snana* (holy bath). According to Hindu tradition, pilgrimage is called a *thirtha yatra*, "a journey to a holy place, referred to as a 'ford' (thirtha), a place for 'crossing over,' where the divine world touches or meets the human world".[12]

Traditionally seven cities are considered as sacred cities for pilgrimage. They are Ayodhya, Mathura, Haridwar, Varanasi, Ujjain, Dwaraka and Kanchipuram. Sacred rivers particularly Ganges, Yamuna, Narmada, Kaveri, and Godavari are given prime importance. Towns located along these rivers, particularly those located on the banks of Ganges attract maximum pilgrims. At Rishikesh, the pilgrims visit several temples and worship the deities there, bath in the sacred river, give alms, attend the religious discourse of holy men, attend the evening *aarti* and join the singing of *bhajans* or *kirtans* etc. People consider the whole town of Rishikesh as holy and during pilgrimage prefer to spend some time in meditation in Rishikesh before they continue to the other holy sites in the Himalayas.

Endnotes

[1] In Hinduism, every family has a family deity called *Kuladevta*, the ancestral tutelary deity, who is the object of devotion. Daily and regular worship of this deity is of utmost importance. There is a bond between this deity and the family.

[2] If an image is not consecrated, the priest or the worshipper may offer prayers of invocation, bidding the Divine to come and be present for the period of worship and letting the Divine leave at the end of the worshipThis is the normal practice at homes. If the rite of consecration of the *murti* is conducted (like in the temples) the image becomes imbued with the permanent presence of God and a priest must be in residence to offer daily *puja*.

[3] Bathing is essential before entering the temple. Many times it is substituted by washing of feet, sprinkling of water over head etc.

[4] Right hand is considered holier than the left hand.

[5] S.N. Giri, 'The Guru in Hindu Tradition', in V. Mataji (ed.), *Christian Ashrams. A Movement with a Future?* Delhi, ISPCK, 1993, p. 123.

[6] Abhishiktananda, *Saccidananda. A Christian Approach to Advaitic Experience*, Delhi, ISPCK, 1974, p. 202.

[7] J. Castellino, *Becoming an Indian Guru-Priest*, Shillong, Vendrame Missiological Institute, 1982, pp. 13-14.

[8] Abhishiktananda, *Guru and Disciple*, London, ISPCK, 1974, p. 10.

[9] D. Smith, *Hinduism and Modernity*, Malden, Blackwell Publishing, 2003, p. 167. Sikh tradition considers Guru as the Supreme Being.

[10] Underhill, M.M., *The Hindu Religious Year*, New Delhi, Asian Educations Services, 2001, pp.112-116.

[11] Gavin Flood, *An Introduction to Hinduism*, New Delhi: Foundation Books, 2004, p.215.

[12] Flood, *An Introduction to Hinduism*, p.212.

Chapter - 2

An Introduction to the Religious Symbols Found in Rishikesh

As you walk through the streets of Rishikesh or along the shores of Ganges you will find lots of Hindu symbols. Every sage or *sannyasi* comes across to you wearing different symbols. Some are white clad some are saffron (gerua) clad, some have marks on forehead, some have long hair while some have shaved off their hair, some have beads around their neck etc. It is important to understand the meaning of such symbols. We shall now look at some of the prominent symbols.

Ochre-Coloured Dhotis, Shawls and Clean-Shaven Head of Monks

As soon as one enters Rishikesh the dhoti and shawl clad monks are seen everywhere. Dhoti is the loose piece of clothing wrapped around the lower half of the body by men and especially by the monks. They are mostly seen in the ashrams. Besides those differences in the colour of their dhotis one can observe several kinds of variation in marks on their body, especially on the forehead. These marks tell us to which sect they are associated.

The ochre colour generally called *gerua* in India is the normal colour worn by sages, ascetics, and hermits. The colour *gerua* is like the fire or the burnt gold. Therefore symbolically the colour tells about the purity of the person who wears it. This person is free from all impurities and will not be inclined to evil ways. He is like gold purified by fire. He is no more attracted to the greeneries of the world. This colour thus becomes the external sign of one's heart. It is symbolic of complete renunciation of any attachment to the world or body. It is the sign of leaving out all vanity all beauty.

Mostly those monks wearing the *gerua* coloured dhotis shave off their hair completely. Generally they belong to the Shaivaite tradition. In Rishikesh most of the classical ashrams come under the Adi Shankaracharya tradition which is basically Shaivaite. The tonsured person tells the world that he is not of this world anymore. He also removes the *chotti* or *Shikha* (the tuft of hair at the back of the head) to show that he is not bound by any of the karmas and rules. People believe that a *chotti* allows the Almighty to pull the person easily from this material world.

However, mostly those who follow the Shaivaite tradition shave off the hair and wear *gerua* while those of Vaishnavite sects grow long hair and wear white coloured dhoti. The white colour in Hinduism is also symbolic of death. Widows wear white while mourning, symbolic of their detachment from the world. Similarly the Vaisnavaite monks wear white, symbolic of their death to this world. Among them especially the students wear yellow which is symbolic of learning and knowledge. The Shaivaites in general are called as *sannyasis* while the Vaishnavites are called *vairagis*. The Shaivites follow rather radical austere practices.

We can also see some *sadhus* and monks with long folded hair called *jata* or long matted hair. This is symbolic of their commitment to ascetic life and lifelong celibacy. Ideally the hair, which is long and unkept, is simply left to grow and mat naturally. Sometimes mats of hair are ritually smeared with mixture of cow dung, cow urine, ashes or/and Ganges river mud and rolled into long strands and left hanging or loosely coiled and tied in a bundle on top of the head[1]. The long *jata* is considered as a sign of Yogi's magical powers or siddhis he has acquired by his tapas. It must be remembered that according to the Hindu mythology, Lord Shiva the ascetic par excellence and the king of all yogis broke the fall of Ganges which was threatening to inundate the world with his long coiled up *jata*. That is why iconographically Ganges is depicted flowing out of Shiva's matted locks.

Some monks after the ritual bathing cover their bodies with sacred ashes. Ashes convey a sense of death and the dissolution of the material world and the ego. Combined with *jata*, ashes symbolise a lack of regard for the body and a rejection of physical beautification. Ashes also symbolize death, cremation, sacrifice and the practice of austerities. The ash used is preferably taken from the cremation ground. Thus it represents the physical death and destruction. Similarly some monks go completely naked or nearly so wearing only a narrow loincloth. It symbolises the rejection of physical comfort, transcendence of attachment to body and signifies the absence of possessions, status, and rank. Sadhu's nakedness does not imply eroticism, but it is the proof of his overcoming the pull of sensual desires and sexual arousal and remains a sign of bodily denial and non-attachment.

Marks on the Forehead: Ash, *Kunkum* and Sandal Paste

There are various sects and sub-sects among Hindus which can be distinguished based on the symbols they use, which ultimately come from the symbols of the deities they worship. We can see such marks on the arms, chests, and foreheads. Some orthodox Hindus wear it always while many wear them only at *puja* or festivals. It is noticeable clearly in the case of monks and *sadhus*. They invariably wear *tilak*- a mark on the forehead. Some apply *tilak* not only on the forehead, but neck, upper arms, forearms, chest, torso, stomach, and shoulder. Some have simple *tilak,* but others have elaborate markings. Some have only sandal paste while some others have *kumkum* and ash etc.

Sandal paste is symbolic of the spiritual life. When rubbed on a hard surface sandal gives out fragrance. Similarly the devotee should not murmur when difficulties arise, but on the other hand, use them as occasions to emanate sweetness and gentleness. If you visit a temple the priest applies a *tilak* on your forehead as a sign of blessings given by the deity.

The style of markings tells something about the sectarian affiliation of the individual as each sect has its own different way of markings. Mostly the horizontal lines, on the forehead show that the person is a follower of *Shaiva* tradition. For them normally the numbers of lines are two or more. Rarely do they add a red dot in the middle or even a crescent moon as well[2]. The vertical lines worn by the devotee depict that he/she is a worshipper of Vishnu and has the allegiance to *Vaishnava* tradition. The number of lines is mostly three for both. The *Vaishnavites* also mark the line in the shape of English letter U, sometimes with a dot or small central line within it. The dot is symbolic of the Supreme Being. When they put the dot with lines either vertical or horizontal, they claim that the Shiva or Vishnu as the Supreme Being. The horizontal lines of *Shaivaites* are white while the dot is red. The worshippers

of *Devi* or followers of *Shakti* tradition apply *kumkum* or the red turmeric powder[3]. They use one vertical line or dot (but not the one worn by the women which is called *bindi*). The ascetics of Vaishnava tradition are identified by their 10 signs. They are "conch and chakra brands burned into the upper arms; shaved heads and face or matted hair and beard; tulsi bead necklace, tilak; guru-mantra containing the name of either Rama or Krishna; top-knot or tuft hair on the upper back of the head; the sacred thread; gourd water-pot; white or yellow cloth; and guru's teachings"[4].

The Rosary or the *Japamala* and the *Likhita Japam*

You can notice devotees or ascetics reciting the mantra with beads. The rosary they use has 108 beads. This number has a specialty. It is said that a man breathes an average of 21600 per day. Therefore if one can say 200 times of rosary a day then it is 21600 times which means he has done one *japa* or mantra for one breath (200x108=21600). In other words, he has remembered God through out the day. There is an additional bead knotted, which is separated from the main rosary called *sumeru*, or *meru*. This represents the guru who has given the mantra. Therefore the guru bead is never crossed while repeating the mantra, but the rosary is turned around and the next round is begun with 108th bead.

You can also see some devotees sitting at the banks of Ganges and writing the name of Lord Rama. This *sadhana* is called *Likhita Japam* which means writing of God's name for one crore (ten million) times known also as ram *koti*. This spiritual ritual is also called writing tapas. This spiritual means is quite simple as it is writing down the name of the Lord in a book. Before writing, the devotee must take bath/shower and write with devotion while orally repeating what he is writing.

Walking Around the Temple

You can also observe the devotees who visit the temple take a walk around the temple or take a circumambulation around the central *murti* of the temple. This walk is called *pradakshina* or *parikrama*. When you do it you keep the *murti* always on your right side. Normally the number of *pradakshina* depends on the main deity of the temple. The general rule is that for male deities, the number of *pradakshinas* should be in 'even' numbers (2, 4, 6) and for female deities, it should be in odd numbers. However, for all gods and goddesses the numbers once, thrice, eleven or twenty-one are acceptable. It symbolically tells that God is the centre of our lives and the devotee acknowledges it while making the *pradakshina*. He or she wants to make sure that always the thoughts and actions will be centered on God.

Achamana and *Prokshana*

If you observe closely the ritual bathing, then you can observe that the holy dip in the river is preceded by sipping of water. This sipping is a ritual called *achamana* which is sipping water thrice while repeating the name of the Lord. It is followed by *prokshana* which is sprinkling water over one's body for the sake of purity when a bath is not possible. It is a purification rite done before all religious ceremonies. Although there are various forms of performing *achamana*, the simplest and most common form is done by taking water in the palms three times and swallowing or sipping it from the base of the thumb while reciting the mantra. As part of this ritual, with the same wet hand one must touch the various parts of the body namely face twice, and eyes, ears, nose, shoulders, breast, and head once. It is advised that one performs *achamana* before any sacred ceremony like sacrifice, *puja*, study of scripture and after meals or visiting crematorium etc. When *achamana* is performed in the river, one must make sure that the water should be above knees and below naval (See our previous section 1.1.).

Bell and OM

One can hear the ringing of bells all the time from the temples in Rishikesh. As devotees enter the temple first they invariably ring the bell. The bell is also used in *pujas* and many other rituals. They also ring the bell during the *aarti*. The primary purpose of devotees to visit the temple is not for *puja* but for the auspicious vision or *darshan* of the deity. This *darshan* is the essential and primary part of any worship. Thus by ringing the bell the devotee is informing the deity that he has come to visit the deity and invokes the attention towards him. Secondly, the sound of the bell is considered auspicious as it can remove the evil. This sound drowns any irrelevant sound from the atmosphere.

Since the sound of the bell is regarded as sound similar to *OM* the universal name for God, most rituals and prayers are started with *OM*. While ringing the bell many would repeat the following *mantra*;

Aagamaarthamtu devaanaam

gamanaarthamtu rakshasaam

Kurve ghantaaravam tatra

devataahvaahna lakshanam

(I ring this bell indicating the invocation of divinity, so that virtuous and noble forces enter (my home and heart); And the demonic and evil forces from within and without, depart.)

Om is a phonetic symbol rather than a word. The idea of Om is mainly based in the Vedic Scriptures. Swami Sivananda considers 'Om as the all-pervading sound that has come out from the essence of God'[5]. The symbolization of Om has a different combination with its sound and meaning. In Hinduism Om is said to be the most sacred of all sounds. It is the syllable which preceded the universe and from which it was created. The Hindu theology states that Om is the root syllable, the cosmic vibration that holds together the atoms of the world and heavens.

The Hindus begin their day or any work or a journey by uttering Om as a prayer. Many Hindus, as an expression of spiritual perfection, wear the sign of Om as an ornament. This symbol is found in every Hindu temple, family temple and even in houses. It is a belief among Hindus that a newly born child is to be guided into the world with this holy symbol. Therefore after birth, the child is ritually cleansed, and the syllable Om is written on its tongue with honey. Thus right at the time of birth the syllable Om is initiated into the life of a Hindu and ever remains with him as the symbol of piety. Om is uttered during the sacrificial acts by the Hindu priests while the common people chant Om in the home during their prayers (especially at the time of *puja*). 'Hari Om' is pronounced in the beginning and at the end of religious ceremonies. It is done in order to remove the impediments that may have caused due to the mis-pronouncements of some mantras[6]. Thus the symbol has entered both into the cultic practice in the religion as well as in popular Hinduism as the most frequently used symbol.

Breaking Coconut

Coconut is particularly important for Hindu *pujas*. Breaking a coconut is a common practice all over India before any auspicious ceremony. Breaking of the coconut represents breaking of the ego. When you break a coconut what comes out is the inner white and water. Similarly when one breaks the ego, your mind also becomes pure white. The water is symbolic of the divine nectar. Thus breaking of one's ego is essential for attaining wisdom and making oneself pure.

Tulsi Plant

Tulsi or the holy basil is a sacred plant that you would find in almost all the traditional Hindu homes. As such having a Tulsi plant at home is considered very auspicious and exhibits the religious bent of the family. A Hindu household is considered incomplete if it does not have a Tulsi plant in the courtyard. Many families have the Tulsi planted in a specially built structure, which has images of deities installed on all four sides, and an alcove for a small earthen oil lamp. Some households are particular to grow up to a dozen Tulsi plants on the courtyard or in the garden forming a 'Tulsi-van'- a miniature basil forest. Tulsi is worshipped in the morning and evening.

Hindus regard Tulsi as an earthly manifestation of the goddess Tulsi/Vrinda and as the avatar of Lakshmi, and the consort of the god Vishnu. The offering of its leaves is mandatory in ritualistic worship of Vishnu. The legends say that Vishnu's spouse, being jealous of her husband's attention to Tulsi, changed her into a plant. However, Vishnu, in order that he might still enjoy her company transformed himself into a Saligrama- an ammonite that is found in some rivers, mostly in Nepal. People who are more religious and who can afford, these Saligrams are carefully kept and preserved as holy living beings.[7] Every year a ceremony of Tulsi vivaha- the ceremonial marriage of the Tulsi plant to the Saligram is conducted. This wedding signifies the end of the monsoon season and the beginning of the wedding season in Hinduism.

Endnotes

[1] R.L. Gross, *The Sadhus of India: A Study of Hindu Asceticism*, New Delhi/Jaipur, Rawat Publications, 1992, p.304.

[2] Deussen, Paul, *Sixty Upanishads of the Veda*, Delhi, Motilal Banarsidass, 1997, pp. 789-790.

[3] Gautam Chatterjee, *Sacred Hindu Symbols*, Delhi, Abhinav Publications, 2003, p.11.

[4] R.L. Gross, *The Sadhus of India: A Study of Hindu Asceticism*, New Delhi/Jaipur, Rawat Publications, 1992, p.376.

[5] Sri Swami Sivananda, *Meditation on Om and Mandukya Upanishad*, Shivanandanagar: The Divine Life Society, 1985, 14.

[6] Dwivedi Bhojraj, *Religious Basics of Hindu Beliefs*, New Delhi, Diamond Books, 2010, pp.34-35.

[7] W.J. Wilkins, *Modern Hinduism*, New Delhi: Cosmo Publications, 1985, p.202.

Chapter - 3

An Introduction to the Ashrams in Rishikesh

Although Rishikesh is popularly known for its ashrams, in reality it is not so. Rishikesh is primarily a place for tapas. The area where many ashrams are located is called Tapovan. It is the forest where an ascetic spends time in ascetical practices. Hence the ascetics from other parts of India also visit the place not to stay in any ashram but to spend time in tapas in the calm and serene atmosphere in the lap of the Ganges, though the serenity is now on the decrease. Before we proceed further let us have clearer a understanding about the very concept and working of ashrams.

The Concept of Ashram

The word *ashram* has been derived from Sanskrit root *sram* which means to make efforts. The meaning of the derived word *ashram* is a state in which one makes efforts on one's own. Sanskrit writers describe *ashrama* or *ashram* as a place where *tapas* (austerities) are performed[1]. Etymologically the Sanskrit word *ashram* has two meanings. The first is that of a religious hermitage or a residence where holy people live and perform religious austerities of prayer, *yoga*, penance etc[2]. In general this word is used to denote this meaning. Secondly the word *ashrama* also refers to a stage of life. According to the Hindu ideal of life, every individual is expected to go through four stages (*ashramas*) of life[3]. "Generally, consecrated life in Hinduism may be understood as one of four spiritual stages of a Hindu. The first two stages are *brahmacharya* (student of Vedic scripture), *grihastha* (householder). When a person's household responsibilities are over (i.e. when he has seen his children's children, and so ensured the continuity of ancestral rites) then come the stage of *vanaprastha* (forest dwelling). Here one leaves the family to dedicate to meditation. The fourth and final stage of a pious Hindu is the *sannyasa* or consecrated life. Here one consecrates himself fully by complete renunciation of everything for the pursuit of realizing the Absolut."[4]

The statement of *All India Consultation on Ashrams'* describe *ashram* "as a place of an intense and sustained spiritual quest, centred on a guru, man or woman recognized by others as a person of deep spiritual experience. In an *ashram* primacy is given to this relentless quest through *sadhana* or specifically Indian spiritual practices. It is a place where above all, people can experience God"[5]. *Ashram* gives the glimpse about the concrete expression of the Indian spiritual quest. "It [*ashram*] is not an institution in the ordinary sense of the term. It is an organism, rather than an organization, and it is admirably suited to the religious conditions of India"[6].

Christian Monastery Compared with Indian Ashram

The Christian monastery and the Indian ashram are not identical, though both of them are places for meditation and renunciation of the world. Christian monasteries have strict rules, structures, and timetables. Every individual is assigned a function and all the members are supposed to take part in all the community activities. The head of the monastery functions as the head of a family and makes decisions concerning most aspects of monastery life. There is mutual love, sharing and interaction. The whole atmosphere is community centred[7]. Well-defined and set prayer-forms and spiritual exercises are prescribed and followed. These spiritual exercises in community are considered as means for God-realization. Mostly the monasteries are part of religious organizations. For the most part the members form one community and spend their whole life in the monastery.

Unlike a monastery, an *ashram* is completely disconnected from larger associations[8]. An *ashram* does not prescribe creedal or denominational tests. It is non-sectarian and un-denominational. No rigid and strict rules and discipline is maintained. It is non-authoritarian and guru does not exercise the authority of an abbot or of the head of a monastery as in the Christian monasteries. He is like an older brother instructing the younger ones in spiritual exercises and discipline[9]. But one imposes strict rules on oneself. Every member is free to follow his or her means of God-realization within the general framework of *ashram*. Any seeker can come and stay for a short period or if he/she wishes as there is the prevalence of informality, which makes it possible for anyone to come and stay as long as they choose. There is no set form of prayer and spiritual exercises prescribed for all. Ample scope is provided for unhurried prayer and reflection and for the deepening of the spiritual life. Values such as *ahimsa* or non-injury, friendliness to all, *asanga* or non-attachment to material things are fostered while discarding the desire for material good and for the fruits of labour[10].

The Location of an *Ashram*

An *ashram* normally gets located in forests or riverbanks away from human habitation, amidst natural surrounding conducive to spiritual instruction and meditation. It gets organized around a guru who has come to the fourth stage of life, and who has "dedicated his life in an extraordinary manner to religious exercise (*shrama*), living, in all likelihood, in areas somewhat removed from villages and towns"[11]. Although such a guru lives in a dwelling away from the cares of the world, soon the disciples who are in search of the advice of such gurus would surround him[12]. An *ashram* gets born when disciples accept the guru by which the place where he was living becomes an *ashram*[13]. So ideally an *ashram* is not founded by the *guru* or by someone. Disciples gather around the guru and live together a communal life. The banks of holy rivers and the hilltops and caves in the forests become the natural choice of the gurus who have already left the cares of the world.

Life in the Ashram

Men and women of different cultures, places, regions, and creeds collect in the *ashram*[14]. Members are linked together by a common desire to discover truth. The common goal is God-realization and realization of oneness with one's fellowmen. Members come together for meals, but they eat in silence. The *ashrams* provide two meals, each one normally consisting of two items, namely *chappaatti* (bread) and *daal* (pulses or lentils). But a good number of seekers are content with one meal[15]. Every *ashram* has a minimum common programme in which all the members are expected to join[16]. Mostly all come together for the morning meditation (from 05.00 to 06.00), noon prayer, the evening *aarti*, the occasional discourse by the *guru* etc.

Special emphasis is laid on a life of silence and meditation[17]. The members spend their time in personal *sadhana* (spiritual practices). Every seeker is supposed to support the *ashram* by his/her manual labour which is called *ashram seva*. There are no interactions between the seekers, but they are free to meet the spiritual guide or the *guru*. Pilgrims and spiritual seekers for a shorter duration of 10 to 15 days are also welcome in any *ashram*. For such seekers, there are more spiritual exercises like common worship, meditation, *yoga*, discourse etc. And to the benefit of such members and for the benefit of general public there is preaching done by the guru or one of the learned *sannyasi*[18].

Ashrams in Ancient and Modern India

Monasticism as we understand today was not part of earlier, even though, religious life called *sannyasa* was one the four stages of life of every individual[19]. Hinduism, throughout history has witnessed too many individual monks who lived either in the forest or in some huts. Hindu *Ashrams* have been powerful religious institutions throughout Hindu history and theology. Most Hindu kings are known to have had a sage who would advise the royal family in spiritual matters and in other matters in times of crisis. Emperors, kings, and rulers barefoot and with great respect approached *rishis* (sages) in their *ashrams* to seek counsel and blessings- a practice being continued even today by the politicians[20]. Most of the religious classics of Hinduism, including the Upanishads were written by the great sages who were leading the life of a monk[21].

Presently in Hinduism religious life is organized under what is called *Sampradaya* which can be roughly translated as 'tradition' or 'religious system'. It is true that one can often see several individual 'freelancer *sadhus* and *sadhvis*' living either in the edges of society or in the banks of holy rivers, wearing ochre robes or naked, shaven head or long and matted hair following their own spiritual practice[22]. Although they are honoured and respected, they lack the social acceptance, spiritual identity and spiritual authority associated with the *Sampradaya*.

It is also generally believed that unless initiated by a spiritual master of a *Sampradaya*, the mantra he recites is without any effect. Moreover, if any religious group or individual cannot prove its or his descent from a recognized *Sampradaya* and a *prampara*, it or he risks being dismissed as illegitimate. One can belong to a *Sampradaya* by taking initiation in a guru-disciple tradition called *parampara*. Thus by receiving initiation into a *parampara* of a living guru, one formally enters a *Sampradaya*. Generally the *Sampradaya* are broadly categorized into three, namely, the Vaishnava, the Shaivaite and the Advaita Vedanta *Sampradaya*. Each of them has its own view of spirituality and discipline and each of them having a major philosopher or Guru as the founder or beginner. To make it simpler, the ascetics can be categorized either as Shaivaite or Vaishnavite. Generally the Shaivaite ascetics are called *sannyasis* or yogis and are primarily devoted to Shiva and the Vaishnavite ascetics are called *Vairagis* or *Bairagis* and worship Vishnu or one of his incarnations[23].

According to the Advaita Vedanta Sampradaya, the great Vedanta philosopher and theologian Adi Shankaracharya (who was a *naishtika bhrahmachari*- a celibate ascetic from childhood) founded monastic centres called *peethas* in four corners of India. They are the Sharada Peeth Sringeri, Karnataka (in the south), Kalinka Peeth, Dwaraka, Gujarat (in the west), Govardhana Peeth, Puri, Orissa (in the east) and Jyotir Peeth, Joshimath, Uttarakhand (in the north). Two *upa peethas* were also established in Kashi and Kanchi. It is generally considered that historically the Shaivaite ascetics were organized by Shankara into what is called Dashnamis, (ten names) in the Ekadandi (one staff) tradition[24].

Besides the Dashnami orders, another major order found in the northern part of India is the Nathapanthis or Kanpatis (a name they got due to their split year- a practice of piercing their ears during initiation) or Gorakhpanthis. They emphasise on hatha yoga and on gaining extra ordinary powers called *sidddhis*. Another major sect is the Lingayaths, a sect almost exclusively located in south India.

Although there has been a proliferation of heterogeneous Vaishnava sects and orders, in the 14th century a conference of Vaishnava religious leaders agreed to a structuring of the many Vaishnava *sampradayas* into the so called *catuh sampradaya*, affiliating each of them with one of four mainstream *sampradayas*: they are Srivaishnava(Ramanuja), Brahma (Madhva) Kumara(Nimbaarka) and Rudra(Vishuswami and vallabha). All later Vaishnava congregations were to seek affiliation with one of these four to be recognised as legitimate. Two however, Chaitanya and Sri Sampradya while nominally affiliated became fairly independent due to the number of followers, and influence. Chaitanya (1485-1533) was the founder of Gaudiya Vaishnava school, which became in the west as ISKON (International Society for Krisna Consciousness).

Ashrams came to the prominence of the Indian society during the Bengal renaissance. It started with Raja Ram Mohan Roy (1775-1833) and ended with Rabindranath Tagore (1861-1941). It was a period of awakening in the Indian society in the field of philosophy, literature, science, religion, and politics, beginning from the province of Bengal and spreading to other parts of India. As part of the renaissance there emerged several reform movements in both religious and social fields. The modern Indian *ashrams* developed as a part of the Renaissance and played a vital role in social and religious renewal[25]. The Sabarmati *ashram* (of M. K. Gandhi), initiated the political regeneration while the educational regeneration came through Shanti Niketan (of R.N Tagore)[26]. Keshab Chandra Sen in 1872 had established an *ashram* in Calcutta, Ramakrishna Paramahansa and his disciple Swami Vivekananda founded the Ramakrishna *ashram*, in 1897. Rabindranath Tagore had established his Shanti Niketan in 1901. When Gandhiji came to India from South Africa he started his freedom struggle from his *ashram* at Sabarmati in 1915. His *ashrams* at Sevagram and at Sabarmati were centres of inspiration and enlightenment for whole of India. The Ramana *ashram* at Tiruvannamalai and the Aurobindo *ashram* founded in 1926 by Aurobindo Ghose at Pondicherry were also important in India. These *ashrams* contributed in combining the religio-cultural activities with a reformation of Hinduism and a myth of a past golden age[27].

Although there are many ashrams in Rishikesh, most of them are not in line with the classical ashrams. I have not included all the ashrams as there are many such ashrams. I have included in this list mostly the important ones with a guru disciple tradition. First, we shall see those ashrams which are in the Adi Shankaracharya tradition. Afterwards I shall also present some other ashrams as well.

Kailash Ashram

Kailash ashram is the mother of all ashrams in Rishikesh as Rishikesh's development is synonymous with the development of this ashram. It was established by honourable Swamiji Dhanraj Giri in the year 1880. Until 18th century, Rishikesh was used as a stop over by the monks on their pilgrimage to char dham. There were no big ashrams or proper resting places in this area. A young ascetic Dhanraj Giri on his pilgrimage arrived at Rishikesh. Seeing the serenity he found it suitable for his tapas. Therefore he made a hut out of grass on the banks of Ganges at Muni ki Reti and performed his meditation. This young monk was well versed in Advaita and his reputation spread around. Hearing the reputation, the king of Tehri came to visit him. The king was taken up by the simple life of Swami Dhanraj Giri, that he offered free land for the construction of an ashram. However, Swamiji was not very keen on establishing an ashram. The disciples also urged the Swamiji to construct something to preserve the good collection of spiritual books he had. Therefore considering the request of the king and the prayers of the disciples, Swamiji agreed to construct a library to properly preserve the books. This library later came to be known as Kailash Ashram. It is also said that Adi Shankaracharya on his way to Joshimat to establish a temple there, stayed on the same small hilltop on which the present Kailash Ashram is situated now.

On his spiritual quest as a student Swami Vivekananda also had stayed with honourable Dhanraj Giri for several months and later recollects the inspiration he received from Swamiji. Even today many monks of Ramakrishna Mission come to Kailash Ashram to study and to be initiated into formal religious life. Rishikesh was the preferred halting centre of thousands of *yogins* and *sannyasins* of diverse sects to assemble every year to spend the winter in reading the scriptures and practicing yoga and meditation. Dhanraj Giri was a celebrated name for his

Evening aarti by inmates at Kailash Ashram

scholarship in Vedanta and for his holy life as a monk. Hence many monks and seekers came from all over India to listen to his discourses and to study under him. Those who came from far often went back to their places to spread the spiritual insights they received from Swami Dhanraj Giri.

The number of disciples increased so much that it was difficult to find place for all in the small ashram. Therefore many disciples made temporary huts with grass in the vicinity and stayed.

Once a rich devotee came to have the darshan of Swami Dhanraj Giri and seeing the gurukula style of teaching and learning Vedanta, he was impressed and he requested the Swamiji to allow him to do some service/something for the Swamiji. But Swamiji replied that he did not need anything, however, he can meet the inmates and if they require anything, he was free to do so. When the inmates were gathered to find out what they wanted, they also said in one voice that they also did not require anything.

A temple was built in the campus during the time of Dhanraj Giri Maharaj. Slowly many more buildings were built and more disciples came to stay in the ashram to study the Hindu scriptures. Today this ashram gives *diksha* (initiation to religious life) to deserving *sadhaks* as monks. It is also known as one of the best centres for studying Sanskrit, Vedanta and other Hindu scriptures.

Brahmanada Ashram

Swami Brahmanad Bharati was a contemporary of Dhanraj Giri Maharaj. Those days there were many disciples coming to study at Kailash Ashram, but not enough room was available at the ashram. To find a solution to this problem Swami Brahmanad Bharati established an ashram at Muni ki reti primarily for the stay of monks who wanted to study under Dhanraj Giri. He called this Brahmanand Ashram and transferred its ownership to Dhanraj Giri.

Kailash Ashram can be called the mother ashram for most of the ashrams in Rishikesh and outside. Many monks of this tradition have travelled to different places and established similar ashrams. There are others who were initiated by Kailash Ashram but started their own ashrams or became heads of other ashrams. Among them are Narisingh Giri Maharaj of Dhruveshwar Math, Swami Tapovan Mahraj often called as the king of Himalayas, Swami Mahadevanand of Bholandanand Ashram, Swami Shivananda of Divine Life Society and Shivananda Ashram, Saccidananda Saraswati of Andhra Ashram and so on.

Today Kailash Ashram stands tall as a leading ashram where Vedanta studies and Hindu scriptural exegesis are carried out. It has become the mark of orthodoxy in the Adi Shankaracharya's Vedanta tradition. It is here those seeking to enter the religious life come to learn and to be initiated.

Swarg Ashram

Swarg ashram is one of the oldest institutions founded in Rishikesh. This ashram was built in memory of Swami Vishudhananda who came to be known as Baba Kala Kamli Wala. In the early 1920s life at Rishikesh was not comfortable. Pilgrims and monks came to Rishikesh mostly on their pilgrimage to Badrinath. It is said that the winter was so chilly that the sages carried fire on their head as they went to the Himalayas. There were no roads and the area was under thick forest. Only the monks and ascetics could survive, eating meagrely when someone provided food or on what was available in the forest. The pilgrims also had to stop at Rishikesh, but they too had no place to rest nor any provisions for food. To help the pilgrims and the sadhus, Swami Vishuddhanandaji went to the little town of Rishikesh and appealed to the rich to construct a halting place for pilgrims at Rishikesh and along the road to Badrinath. He also appealed to them to offer free food to the sadhus. Swami Vishudhanandaji was a holy man and always wore a black blanket. Therefore people fondly called him Baba Kala Kamli Wala (the black blanket clothed monk). His effort succeeded in providing free food and accommodations to the pilgrims and ascetics. One of the disciples of Swami Vishuddhanandaji, called Atmaprakashanandaji Maharaj, moved to the eastern side of Ganges and settled down there and that location came to be known as Swarg Ashram and he opened an *annakshetra* or free kitchen for the resident ascetics over the area.

However this ashram at present does not function as a classical ashram with a spiritual head and disciples but is under a Trust which manages it. There are many residential cottages small and big, meant for sadhus, saints and travellers. Besides these, there are also dharmashalas for pilgrims and devotees. The free kitchen provides food for the ascetics and poor twice a day. There is also a library with plenty of spiritual books and periodicals. With the help of donors a good mango tree garden is also maintained in the ashram *kshetra*. It also has several shopping stores, dispensaries, restaurants, and hotels for travellers.

Sivananda Ashram

Swami Sivananda Maharaj arrived in Rishikesh in 1922 and stayed in a small kutir (hut) of Swarg ashram, at the banks of Ganges where he practiced tapas (austerities). He received *diksha* (initiation) from Swami Vishvanandji Maharaj of Kailash Ashram in 1924 and became his *diksha* guru while Swami Vishnudevanandji Maharaj was his sannyas kriya guru. For the next 12 years he performed his strict *tapasya*, mostly on the other side of Ganges to avoid the visitors. However slowly the austerity of Swamiji began to spread to people and on their pilgrimage to Badrinath they started to visit him. One of the devotees who came to Swarg Ashram took *sannyasa* with the name Swami Hariomananda Saraswati and became an associate and a disciple of Sivananda. A few more associates also joined him.

A Monk at the Sivananda Ashram

Due to social and other reasons, they felt it necessary to shift their residence from Swarg Ashram. In 1936 Gurudev as he was fondly called, together with associates crossed the Ganges and cleaned up an abandoned cowshed and occupied it. The close associates with him were Swami Swarupanand, Swami Atmanand and Swami Advaitanand. It gradually expanded as the number of disciples increased. The small hut was called Ananda Kutir. It is the beginning of Sivananda ashram and the Divine Life Society. They had to walk every day to Rishikesh for food which they received from the Baba Kali Kambli wala.

The trio of Swami Swarupanand, Swami Advaitanand and Swami Atmanand went on a *sankirtan* tour of North India. It was Swami Swarupanand who translated into Hindi the lectures or discourses of Gurudev who mostly delivered it in English. This spiritual *sankritan* tour would last for months. During such a tour in Ambala, some people suggested to Gurudev that they be organized in an official manner and a proposal was put forward to form an organized society. Swami Sivanandji said "Do it now". Thus the deed of registration was written and registered in Ambala making the Divine Life Society registered in Punjab. Soon a centre for pulsing also was created with the support of Bengali devotees who started to publish the works of Gurudev.

In 1953 Swami Sivananda organized the World Parliament of Religions at Sivananda Ashram. Prior to that he had already organized the All World Religious Federation in 1945 and All World Sadhus Federation in 1947 and established the Yoga Vedanta Forest Academy in 1948 which gives systematic spiritual training to resident seekers. He left his body in 1963.

Sivananda Ashram has the tradition of celebrating the festivals of all religious affiliations. At Christmas eve students from Samanvaya sing carols at the Christmas gathering conducted in the ashram. Even the very ashram temple called Viswanath temple has idols of several deities besides Lord Shiva the presiding deity. The ashram has meditation hall, temples, lecture halls, hospital and living compartments. Swami Sivananda and his disciple Swami Chidananda have written many books on spiritual life.Sivananda Ashram has the tradition of celebrating the festivals of all religious affiliations.

Sivanand Samadhi

At Christmas eve students from Samanvaya sing carols at the Christmas gathering conducted in the ashram. Even the very ashram temple called Viswanath temple has idols of several deities besides Lord Shiva the presiding deity. The ashram has meditation hall, temples, lecture halls, hospital and living compartments. Swami Sivananda and his disciple Swami Chidananda have written many books on spiritual life.

Today the Divine Life Society is a worldwide organization with more than 300 branches around the world, of which Sivananda Ashram is the guiding light. It is an open ashram welcoming people from all walks of life. It is a non-sectarian institution committed to 'being good and doing good'. Anyone interested in leading a serious spiritual life is welcome here. Not many are given initiation but only to limited number of inmates or who the branches sent to be initiated. However many people come to the ashram for a short period of stay and get initiated to *mantra diksha*.

Dayananda Ashram

Dayananda Ashram was established by Swami Dayananda Saraswati in the 1960s. He was called Natarajan before taking up *sannyasa*. In association with Swami Chinmayananda, he set up Arsha Vidya Gurukulam to spread the message of Vedanta where people take up renunciation and spread the Vedic message. The Arsha Vidya Peetham or Gurukulam is a chain of centres spread around the country. In the year 1962 he accepted *sannyasa* from Swami Chinmayananda. Thereafter, he went to Mumbai to the newly inaugurated Chinmaya Mission branch 'Sandeepany'. There he taught the chanting of Bhagavad Gita and the Upanishads to the students at Sandeepany.

In 1963 he moved to a grass hut in Purani Jhari, Rishikesh and spent time in studies in Brahma Sutras under Swami Tarananda Giri at Kailash Ashram. When Swami Chinmayananda's health deteriorated, the public lectures in Gita and Upanishads in different towns and cities were given by Swami Dayanand Saraswati. He was a vocal opponent of religious conversion and tried to bring all the Hindu religious heads together to defend Hinduism. In 1971 he developed a three-year residential Vedanta coursefor the Sandeepany and conducted it twice from 1972 and 1979. This course is now offered at Swami Dayananda Ashram Rishikesh. Besides these lengthy residential courses on Vedanta and other sacred texts meant for serious seekers and aspirants to *sannyasa*, there are also short-term courses offered. They also teach Sanskrit and Vedic chants, besides the daily discourse on the Upanishads in the Advaitic tradition.

Yog Niketan

Yog Niketan was started in 1964 by yoga Guru Swami Yogeswarananda Saraswati Maharaj with the intention of spreading yoga. Hence the main activity of the ashram is spreading the eight-fold path of Patanjali Yoga.

Besides the daily Hatha yoga and Raja yoga classes, daily discourse on Hindu philosophy and theology are also offered at the centre. The lecture is followed by questions and answers. The students and guests are also free to attend the daily *havan - agnihotra* or fire ritual conducted in the morning.

Shri Avdhoot Ashram

Following the Gheesa Sant tradition, Shri Avdhoot ashram was established by Sri Chandan Dev Avdhootji Maharaj and his close associate and follower Sri Raghuwar Dayal Shastri

Shankhya Yog Vedantacharyaji in 1961. The present head of the ashram is Shri Akhandanandji who offers daily *satsanghs* on Upanishads especially on Bhagavad Gita from 9.00 to 10.00 am. He is a famous scholar in Vedanta tradition in the Adi Shankaracharya School.

This ashram offers training in traditional Ashtanga and Hatha yoga. Besides these, the ashram also feeds the poor and the ascetics. Other charitable activities are also initiated by the ashram.

Neuro Rehabilitation Centre

Avdhoot ashram also offers free treatment to those suffering from spinal injury, neurological problems, and various paralysis cases. The treatment is done with a combination of the traditional medicines as well as advanced technology together with physiotherapy.

Swami Swatantranand Ashram

Swami Swatantranand Ashram is situated at Sheesham Jhari, near Swami Dayanand Saraswati Ashram. Swami Swatantranand was born in 1950 in Itawa U.P, as the youngest child in the family and was called Jagdish Narayan. As a young man he was compassionate to the poor and Dalits in the society. Therefore he started to add 'manav' which means human to his name which made him known as manav. As time went by, he met J.P. Narayan and later with Vinova Bhave at Pavnar, Wardha. While studying Vedas at Chinmaya Mission Bombay he encountered Swami Dayanand Saraswati who initiated him as Brahmachari Swatantra Chetan. Thereafter he went round teaching Vedanta. In 1985 at Haridwar he was initiated into religious life as Swami Swatantrananda Saraswati, by Swami Dayanad Saraswati.

In 1998 he met Sri Sri Ravi Shankar of the Art of Living Foundation. Thereafter, Swami Swatantrananda also became a messenger of the Art of Living. It was in 1991 that he laid foundation stone at Rishikesh for his ashram, which was completed in one year. This ashram conducts occasional discourses on Gita and meditation. They also conduct occasional courses of Art of Living.

Omkarananda Ashram

Omkarananda Ashram was established in 1967. As a young boy Jayanarayana left his home in South India for Himalayas. He met Swami Sivananda who called him *bala yogi* and *bala jnani.* Sivananda initiated him to religious life at an early age of seventeen. He also learned under Swami Nityananda the secrets of Tantra Yoga. Omkarananda was a prolific writer. He published his first book (The Story of an Eminent Yogi) in 1947 in the same year he was given *sannyasa disksha* by Sivananda. Thereafter he has authored several books. Before he had started his own ashram, he had worked as the right hand of Swami Sivananda for several years. Today this ashram runs several social and educational activities. These are carried out through two registered charitable trusts. At present Swami Vishveshwaranada Saraswati whom Omkarananda selected as the successor is the president of these societies and functions as the head of the ashram.

Yog Sadhan Ashram

This is one of the earlier ashrams in Rishikesh. It was founded by Yog Yogeshwar Maha Prabhu Sri Ram Lalji Maharaj who was born in 1888. As a young man he went in search of wisdom and a genuine yogic guru. During these journeys he visited several gurus and saints. After several years of search, he reached

Himalayas. It is believed that he was initiated into the secrets of ashtanga yoga and given him the *siddhis* (powers) of yoga by his Satguru Maha Prabhu Vishwa Nath Ji from Nepal. He returned to Punjab and established the institution Yog Sadhan Ashram to spread the mission of yoga. Together with his disciple Sri Swami Mulakh Raj Maharaj he established its branches at Amritsar, Lahore, Rishikesh and Haridwar. His disciple Shri Chaman Lal Kapur Ji Maharaj guides the movement at Hishiapur Punjab.

Yog Sadhan Ashram Rishikesh, has inspired many saints. Several heads of the ashrams have spent time at this ashram. Those include, Swami Sivananda, Avdhoot Daroga Babaji and many others.

Madhuban Ashram

This is a centre for Vaishnava *Bhakti* (devotion). This ashram is situated at Muni ke Reti near Kailash ashram. Since not many Vaishnava ashrams are found in these areas, this ashram functions as the centre for them in this region. The present spiritual head of the ashram is Swami Bhaktiyog Mahraji. This ashram spread the message of *bhakti* and helps devotes to develop Krishna consciousness. A beautiful temple dedicated to Sri Radha Govindji is constructed in the campus where the chanting of '*Hare* Krishna' is conducted uninterrupted. This is a branch of the International Society for Krishna Consciousness (ISKCON). They also teach the congregational chanting of the holy names of God.

Sacha Dham

The ashram with most appeal to foreign pilgrims, the Sacha Dham Ashram was founded by Sri Hans Raj Maharajji. This ashram which is in the line of the Vaishnava tradition is situated on the banks of Ganges at Laxman Jhula. Hans Raj Maharajji had several disciples in the west. Two of his prominent disciples are Shanti Mayi and Prem Baba. During the winter they come to Sacha Dham and deliver *satsanghs*. Prem Baba is from Brazil and Shanti Mayi is from Oregon, U.S.

Beatles Ashram/Maharshi Mahesh Yogi Ashram

Once known as the Beatles ashram, since the Beatles stayed here and wrote songs for their famous White Album, is now in ruins. They stayed here in the ashram of Guru Maharshi Mahesh Yogi which was surrounded by forest and composed songs and the world's attention was drawn to Rishikesh. Maharishi Mahesh Yogi developed the Transcendental Meditation (TM) technique and popularized it.

Before his death in 2008, there were hundreds of TM training centres in India and abroad. Today it is a deserted place which once in its high day housed up to 800 spiritual seekers. In 1997 this ashram was officially closed, and its ownership was taken back by the forest department. However, people do have access to the building with permission.

Beatles Ashram

Swami Rama Sadhaka Grama Ashram

The Swami Rama Sadhak Grama or the village of spiritual seekers was founded in 2002 by Swami Ved Bharati. This centre aims at teaching the Himalayan yoga meditation as interpreted by Swami Rama and guided by his disciple Swami Ved Bharati. Swami Rama was raised in the legendary Himalayan mountain caves. However it was Swami Ved Bharati who founded the Sadhak Grama and gave it the present shape. At present Swami Ritavan Bharati is the spiritual guide and guru of the ashram. This ashram is primarily a centre for yoga and meditation following the Himalayan tradition. They offer regular schedule of hatha yoga, relaxation, breathing practices, meditation, and yoga philosophy for all seekers with personal attention. They also have short and long international certification teacher training programme for yoga teachers.

World yoga day celebrations at Sadhak Grama Ashram

Paramarth Niketan

Paramarth Niketan is one of the favourites among the pilgrims. Foreign tourists, especially from the eastern countries prefer to stay at this ashram. Thisgorgeous ashram was built in 1942 by Swami Shukdevanand. Under the banner of Shukdevanand trust, this ashram undertakes several charitable, cultural, and spiritual activities. One of the important things to be noted is that this is not an ashram meant for monks but for lay people. It has good facilities for accommodating a good number of visitors and pilgrims. At least there are 1000 rooms at their disposal. All the visitors are expected to participate in the morning one-hour prayer starting at 5.00 am. The ashram also conducts regular *satsanghs* in the morning and noon and the recital

Evening Bhajan at Paramarth Niketan

of Gita and Ramayana in the afternoon and evening. They have a famous Ganga *aarti* ceremony in the evening at sunset mostly around 6.00 pm. The evening *aarti* ceremony is a spiritual exercise with *puja* and several *bhajans* followed by the *aarti* to Ganges in which many pilgrims participate.

During the summer they arrange the discourse on Bhagavatham and Ramayan by several famous gurus. Besides conducting several other programs of inter-religious and inter-cultural nature since few years, in collaboration with the Uttarakhand government, they conduct the International Yoga Week festival from March 1 to 7. This ashram also runs a Sanskrit school in the ancient Indian *guru kula* style where education is given until Acharya (MA) stage. The students who are called *munikumars* are given residential facility free of cost. The present head of the ashram Swami Chidanand Saraswati 'muniji' maharaj, is the one who has popularized the Ganga *aarti* in several places. He also conducts several programs for keeping the Ganges and the Himalayas clean and green.

Gita Bhavan

This ashram and temple is situated on the banks of Ganges on the eastern side. This beautiful temple and ashram were constructed in 1944 by a Rajasthani devotee known as Jaylal Goyenka who visited Rishikesh every year for mediation, pilgrimage and prayer. On one of his visits he stayed in Rishikesh for a longer period. He understood the difficulty of pilgrims who wanted to stay overnight to attend the discourse or *satsanghs*. He wanted to find a solution to this problem on a permanent basis. Therefore with the help of his younger brother Harikrishnan Lal Goenka, he purchased the land and constructed a satsangh bhavan. This beautiful place has 1350 rooms and a facility to accommodate around six thousand pilgrims and devotees. The verse from Gita, or Ramayana and Mahabharata are engraved in the walls and stones in the Gita bhavan, besides the painting from the scenes of Gita and other Holy books. The ashram provides free lodging to the devotees. Regular *satsanghs* and recitation of holy books are conducted throughout the year, especially during the festival days. The tall 'Ram naam stambh' constructed at the banks of Ganges has three crores of hand written names of Ram inscribed on it.

Vanamali Ashram

Vanamali Gita Yogashram is a small ashram (spiritual retreat and place of aspiration) poised on the cliff overlooking the Ganges at Tapovan Rishikesh. This ashram was started by Sri Matha Devi Vanamali. Brahmachari Mohan helps in the running the Ashram.

Vanamali Mataji offers meditation, yoga asanas and talks on the Srimad Bhagavad Gita. Devotees and seekers can also participate in these *satsanghs* and other devotional chanting, *Puja* and *aarti*. The course of instruction offered by Vanamali Ashram is designed to follow the ancient rules of harmonious living as expounded by Lord Krishna to Arjuna in the Srimad Bhagavad Gita. Before settling in Rishikesh, Mataji had visited several spiritual centres all over India.

Vanamali Mataji has published quite a few books on the life of Lord Krishna, and yoga. Mataji received *mantradiksha* from Shankaracharya of Kanchi Kamkoti Sri Jayendra Saraswati who visited the ashram on his pilgrimage to Badrinath. As *Gurudaskhina* she offered a plot of her land where according to his wishes replicas of the famous temples of Badrinath and Kedarnath are built. He also said that those who cannot take up a long journey to Kedarnath and Badrinath could gain the same benefits by visiting these two replica temples dedicated to Badri Narayana and Kedarnath.

Vashishta Guha/Swami Purushottamanand Ashram

This is an ancient cave about which mythology says that the great sage Vashishta performed severe penance here 3000 years ago. Sage Vashishta is one of the 7 immortal sages/rishis (saptarishis) in Hindu mythology. Along with his wife Arundhati, he performed tapas here.

Vashishta Cave

This cave is deep dark and high, going further back into the hillside,'[28] a small statue of Lord Shiva in meditation is just visible by the light of a single wick, burning with an almost invisible flame'. Inside the cave there is raised platform or slam enough for a few people to sit down comfortably for a silent meditation. This one of the best places for a silent time if one is interested in spending a day of silence and meditation. This is situated about 20 km away from Tapovan on the Badrinath road. This is also called Swami Purushottamanda Ashram after Swami Purushottama of Ramakrishna Mission, Kerala, arrived in 1928 and made it his home after cleaning it up. He stayed in the cave for 25 years performing his spiritual austerities. Thereafter a room was built for him. After his passing in 1961 this is being run by Sri Chaitanyanandji. In the middle of hush green jungle it is completely a silent and serene place. Visitors and pilgrims come here to sit in silent meditation.

The nearby Arundhati Guha is also popular among many spiritual seekers. This small cave is sometimes referred to as 'Jesus Cave' due to the history of having had visions of Jesus Christ here. Swami Ramdas stayed in the Arundhati Cave on his spiritual pilgrimage (1922-31) and he received the vision of Jesus which he records in his book The Vision of God.

Mr. Joseph, a pilgrim from Kerala, meditating inside the Vashishta cave

Endnotes

[1] H. Ralston, *Christian Ashrams. A New Religious Movement in Contemporary India,* Lewiston/Queenston, The Edwin Mellen Press, 1987, p. 42.

[2] G.S. Ghurye, *Indian Sadhus,* Bombay, The Popular Book Depot, 1953, p. 16.

[3] According to some earlier texts of Hinduism, the four stages are also considered as four *ashramas* and regarded not as temporary stages of a person's life but as four alternate and permanent modes of life open to an individual, and an individual may freely choose only one. See for detail P.

Olivelle, *The Asrama System. The History and Hermeneutics of a Religious Institution*, New York/Oxford, Oxford University Press, 1993, pp. 73-111. See also G.S. Ghurye, *Indian Sadhus*, p. 89. Here we find some kind of a similarity in the four types of monks classified by St. Benedict in the first chapter on the rule of St. Benedict. The first kind is called 'cenobites', who live in a monastery, where they serve under a rule and an abbot. The second kind called 'anchorites' are those who, after their long training under an abbot or monastery pursuing their spiritual life alone. The third kind of monks called 'landlopers' are those living by twos and threes together or even alone, who have no prior experience of a monastery or the rule of a superior. And the fourth class of monks are called 'gyrovagues', who keep going from one province or monastery to another. Benedict condemns the last two types.

[4] M. Ezhaparampil, *Formation to Discipleship*, Claretian Publications, Bangalore, 2004. p.108.

[5] Quoted in S. Painadath (ed.), *Solitude and Solidarity*, Delhi, Ashrama Aikya/ISPCK, 2003, p. 154.

[6] E. Ashirvatham, *Christianity in the Indian Crucible*, Calcutta, YMCA Publishing House, 1957, p. 174.

[7] The desert Fathers were living in the desert and were living alone as hermits. The Carthusians and the Trappists are hermits living in community.

[8] Cf., J.P. Schouten, *Jesus as Guru. The Image of Christ among Hindus and Christians in India*, Amsterdam/ New York, Rodopi, 2008, p. 164.

[9] Ashirvatham, *Christianity in the Indian Crucible*, p. 175.

[10] Ashirvatham, *Christianity in the Indian Crucible*, p. 150.

[11] P. Olivelle, *The Asrama System. The History and Hermeneutics of a Religious Institution*, New York/Oxford, Oxford University Press, 1993, p. 19.

[12] Cf., V. Mataji, *Gurus, Ashrams and Christians*, Madras, The Christian Literature Society, 1980, p. 41.

[13] V. Mataji, 'Finding Our Roots before We Take Wing', in V. Mataji (ed.), *Christian Ashrams. A Movement with a Future?* Delhi, ISPCK, 1993, p. 7.

[14] Tyagimai, 'The Role of the Guru and the Ashram in the Hindu Tradition', in V. Mataji (ed.), *Shabda Shakti Sangan*, Rishikesh, Jeevan Dhara Sadhana Kutir,1995, p. 147.

[15] Ghurye, *Indian Sadhus*, pp. 250-251.

[16] For example, at Shivanada *ashram*, Bihar(the Bihar school of Yoga) the young members rise at five and are kept very busy, in gardening, in cultivating and preparing food, in publishing and printing in accounting, in teaching, learning or research in various forms of yoga. See Ralston, *Christian Ashrams*, p. 65

17 Asirvatham, *Christianity in the Indian Crucible*, p. 149.

18 G.S. Ghurye, *Indian Sadhus,* Bombay, The Popular Book Depot, 1953, p. 250.

19 Every individual has to undergo the four stage of life i.e. student life, house holder, retired life and religious life, while earning the four *purusharthas* in these stages respectively.

20 F. Wilfred, *Beyond Settled Foundations. The Journey of Indian Theology*, Madras, Department of Christian Studies University of Madras, 1999, p. 43.

21 A. Karokaran, *Evangelization and Diakonia*, Bangalore, Dharmaram Publications, 1978, p. 186.

22 Flood, *An Introduction to Hinduism*, p.92.

23 R. L, Gross, *The Sadhus of India: A Study of Hindu Asceticism*, New Delhi/Jaipur, Rawat Publications,1992, p.52.

24 The ten orders are Aranya, Giri, Ashrama, Bharati, Parvatha, Puri, Saraswati, Sagara, Thritha and Vana. Even before Shankara, there were ascetics who were grouped into four, of which two groups carried three staffs called *Tridandis* (the Kutichakas and Bahudakas), one group carried only one staff called *Ekadandis* (the Hamsas) and the last group (Paramahamsas) renounced their staff altogether. There are other Shaivaite groups that pursue physical, martial training or go to the extremes in showing their disdain for normal life. Some like the **nagas** go completely naked, their bodies besmeared with ashes; others like **aghoris** live near creation grounds.

25 R.W. Taylor, *Acknowledging the Lordship of Christ*, Delhi, ISPCK, 1992, p. 53. See also P.M. Collins, *Context, Culture and Worship. The Quest for Indian-ness,* Delhi, ISPCK, 2006c, p. 79.

26 P. Chenchiah, 'The Church and the Indian Christian', in D.M. Devasahayam & A.N. Sudarisanam (eds.), *Rethinking Christianity in India*, Madras, A.N. Sudarisanam, 1935, p. 100. What is in the parenthesis is added by the present researcher.

27 Taylor, *Acknowledging the Lordship of Christ*, p. 53. See also Collins, *Christian Inculturation in India*, p. 79.

28 Vandana, *Gurus, Ashrams and Christians,* Bombay: St. Paul Publications, 1978, p.103

Chapter - 4

An Introduction to the Important Temples in Rishikesh

Bharat Mandir

The oldest temple in Rishikesh is the **Bharat Mandir**, at the old town near Triveni ghat. Some scriptures like Mahabharat and Puranas make a mention about this temple. Many myths and stories also surround this temple. People say that the five Pandavas and Draupadi visited this temple on their way to heaven. It is believed that Lord Ram's younger brother Bharat performed deep penance in this site because of which the temple is named after him. It is said that during the reign of Ashoka, this temple was

Sri Rishikesh Narayan, Bharat Mandir

converted to a Buddhist centre. Some people consider this temple existing from 8ᵗʰ century when Adi Shankaracharya installed the presiding deity in the temple while others believe that the temple came into existence only in the 12ᵗʰ century. However, Rishikesh town grew with this temple. A walk around the temple would give you an idea of how the ancient centre of Rishikesh looked. All the commercial activities were originally around this temple. The statue of God Narayan (Vishnu), which is carved in black stone, is enshrined in the temple. This temple is dedicated to Vishnu, but there are also statues related to Lord Shiva as well. Every year on the day of Vasant Panchami the idol of Lord Hrishikesh Bharatji is taken out in procession for a holy dip in the waters of Ganges. This yearly procession of the temple deity is attended by thousands of people. This feast is celebrated in remembrance of the event of reinstallation of the *murti* in 9ᵗʰcentury by Adi Shankaracharya. The *murti* which was concealed in the maya kund (a pond) in order to save it from Buddhist invasion was installed by him on a Vasant Panchami.

There is also another belief related to this temple. If anyone takes out 108 times of circumambulation of this temple on the day of the feast of Akshaya Tritiya (mostly at towards the end of April), then he or she will receive supreme bliss. This circumambulation or *parikrama* is a substitute even for the pilgrimage to char dhams namely Badrinath, Kedarnath, Gangotri and Yamunotri. Inside the sanctuary of the temple at the upper dome of the temple lies the Sri Yantra which according to the tradition was installed at the entrance by Adi Shankaracharya. The Sri Yantra is a form of mystical diagram, normally associated with the Tantra school. Nine interlocking triangles radiate out from the centre point to form this diagram.

Shankaracharya installed this to harmonize and bring together the various worship schools of the time.

Adjacent to the temple there is an old tree, in fact a combination of three trees grown together. They are Banyan tree, Peepal tree and Bael tree. The broken statue of Buddha kept under the tree was excavated from the site and believed to be at the time of Ashoka when Buddhism spread throughout India. This ancient statue of Buddha sitting in meditation reminds the importance of Rishikesh as the centre for meditation and tapas from ancient times. The other statues from the excavation are preserved in the small museum in the temple campus.

Adjacent to the temple on the south stands the temple of Pataleshwar Mahadev. This is one of the important Shiva temples from the five at Rishikesh. On the west side stands the Bhadra Kali temple dedicated to Mother Durga. Thus we have the three temples at one site presenting the harmony among the three traditions of Shaivism, Vaishnavism and Shaktism.

Shatrughna Temple

Shatrughna temple is said to be established in the 11th century, although some people would date its establishment to the 9th century. It is situated at Muni ki Reti near Ram Jhula. It is also known as Adi Badrinarayan temple. A beautiful *ghat* is constructed in its premises closer to the auto stand near Ram Jhula which is used as the starting point for crossing the Ganges using a boat.

Lakshman Mandir

The third ancient temple is the Lakshman Mandir at Tapovan side of Lakshman Jhula. Legends say that the temple is situated at the very site where Lakshman, the brother of Lord Ram, sat to practice austerities to get rid of his leprosy.

Other Important Temples

Another important temple is the **Terah Manzil** temple which is also known as Kailash Niketan temple situated at the Laxman Jhula. It is a 13 storeyed structure of which each floor has many small temples or altars dedicated to various Hindu gods and goddesses. Unlike other temples, this is not dedicated to a single deity. Tourists love to take photos and selfies in front of this landmark temple. The temple attracts huge crowds during the Mahashivaratri festivals. It is believed that it was established in the 9th century. This temple, together with the Laxaman Jhula becomes the iconic centre for visitors and tourists to take a photo as a souvenir. The Laxman Jhula, the suspension brined across the Ganges, is believed to be constructed at the same place, where according to legends, Lord Laxman had constructed a jute bridge to cross the river. The present ridge was constructed by the British in the year 1929 and opened for public a year later. Currently the bridge is closed for vehicles and allows only a limited number of pedestrians at a time.

Raghunath Temple is located near Triveni Ghat Rishikesh. This temple is dedicated to Lord Ram and his consort Sita. The temple premise has a small holy pond called **Rishikund** which means the pond of the sage. The image of the temple is always visible as a reflection in this pond. There are several myths related to this pond. It is believed that this pond was made by Saint Kabuz who was blessed by Goddesses Yamuna who filled this pond with water. Some people believe that Lord Ram used to take bath in this pond during his exile. Another one says that River Ganges meets River Yamuna at this place.

Rishikund

The **Sri Radha Govindji** temple is also an attractive temple. This temple is founded by the ISKON and throughout the day the chanting of Lord Krishna's name is done. Besides these, there are hundreds of temples and idols on either side of Ganges and in the city.

Sri Neelkant (the blued throated one) **Mahadev** Temple is one of the important holy shrines of the Hindu devotees and pilgrims. This temple is dedicated to Lord Shiva. Situated amidst thick forest on a height of 1330 meters above sea level and 13 kilometres of trekking from Rishikesh, this temple is a favourite

Neelkant Mahadev Temple

of the kawarias. Concerning this temple the legend says that it is where Lord Shiva consumed the poison which originated when the gods and demons (devas and asuras) churned the ocean (samudramanthan) to obtain amrita. Shiva drank the poison in an act to protect the universe, but he stopped the poison at the throat due to which his throat turned blue. This temple is considered a place for achievement of capabilities (*siddhi stal*).

Kunjapuri Devi temple is located about 25 kms away from Rishikesh and at a height of 1676 m. above sea level. Legend says that this temple is situated at the place the body parts of goddesses Sati fell as Lord Shiva was carrying her dead body in his hands. The chest of Goddesses fell at this place. Wherever the body parts fell are called Shakti Peeths (centres of power). Goddesses Sati later incarnated as Goddess Parvati. There are three Shakti Peeths in Tehri district. Once you climb those steep steps to the temple, an overwhelming panoramic view of the snow-capped Himalayan peaks awaits you. One can also have a panoramic view of Rishikesh, Haridwar and Dehradun from here.

Understanding the Temple worship

The important thing is that the temple is not a place of worship but is a place or abode or a sanctuary of God. There are no liturgical services conducted for the whole community or congregation and there are no sacraments initiated or administered in the temple[1]. Mostly the temples are hereditarily owned by families or trusts[2]. Every temple is dedicated to one primary god and the *murti* (image) of this god is placed in the prominent place called *garbha griha*. Other images or *murtis* are also placed in the temple.

The deity is treated mostly like a king. The priest before dawn awakens the *murti* with music and light. Then the *murti* is bathed, dressed, given food, garlanded, *aarti* performed in front and is now ready to give audience/*darshan* to pilgrims and devotees[3]. The deity is offered water for washing the feet and given meals three times, mostly rice and fruit of which he eats the subtle part, leaving the gross material food for his worshippers, or to be given to the poor[4]. Three times the priests offer worship usually at sunrise, noon and in the evening. By noon, the *murti* is put to rest and the pilgrims are not given *darshan*. In the evening at dusk *aarti* is performed and the deity is left to sleep[5].

There is no formal obligation for Hindus to visit the temple[6]. Only very few devotees visit the temple daily. Otherwise, the temples are visited on special occasions, for special needs and for making special requests.

Worship or *puja* is primarily a matter between the individual and deity. "Despite the social experience, the *puja* remains primarily a matter between the individual and the deity, even if the priest stands between"[7]. Even when a large crowd gathers, each person worships the deity all by himself. As one enters the temple after removing the shoes, one rings the bell to rouse the attention of the deity towards him/her. The *puja* has three important aspects. The first is the *darshan* i.e. seeing the deity, which is the most important part. The mutual sight of the believer and God is considered the central part of *puja*[8]. Normally the Hindus do not say that they are going to the temple for sacrifice, worship or prayer but for *darshan*. The second aspect of the *puja* is offering, where the devotee offers something to God in the form of flowers, sweets, or food (this is called *puja*). This is usually done on special occasions. The third is retrieving a part of what is offered called *prasada*, and consuming it. The worshiper gives the offering to the priest, bows before the image, takes a clockwise circumambulation called *pradakshina* around the *murti* and at the end receives from the priest a little part of the offering (*prasada*)[9]. The *prasada* is mostly taken home to share it with family members.

People take different types of vows for gaining material and other benefits. Many votaries promise acts of self-mortification, such as walking round the temple a fixed number of times, covering the distance to the temple by continuous prostrations, taking their food without water, salt, etc., giving away the hair at the shrine and so on.

Endnotes

[1] R. Antoine, 'Rituals and Worship', in R. Antoine (ed.), *Religious Hinduism. A Presentation and Appraisal*, Allahabad, St. Paul Publications, 1968, p. 157.

[2] There are also temples run by trust and owned by government etc.

[3] S. Nikhilananda, *Hinduism. It's Meaning for the Liberation of the Spirit*, London, George Allen & Unwin Ltd, 1958, p. 170.

[4] A.L. Basham, *The Wonder that was India*, London, Sidwick & Jackson, 1968, Reprint, p. 338.

[5] Antoine, 'Rituals and Worship', p. 157.

⁶ K.K. Klostermaier, *A Survey of Hinduism*, New York, State University of New York Press, 1989, p. 307.

⁷ A. Michaels, *Hinduism. Past and Present*, trans. Barbara Harshav, Princeton, Princeton University Press, 1998, p. 245.

⁸ *Ibid.*, p. 230.

⁹ Antoine, 'Rituals and Worship', p. 158. Always the *murti* is at the right side of the person while the circumambulation is taken. Some people repeat it three times.

Chapter - 5

An Introduction to the Yoga Centres in Rishikesh

Rishikesh is one of the most prominent yoga centres in India. There are several institutes, ashrams, centres, and individuals who offer yoga courses, certified yoga teacher trainings and all kinds of yoga retreats. It is exceedingly difficult to select some centres as there are several yoga institutes and centres. Besides the yoga centres, the ashrams also give yoga classes and retreats. In this section I shall limit to only few of the centres. After giving a brief note about yoga, I shall list some of the prominent and trusted yoga centres. Finally, I shall give a detailed description of how and what a yoga centre offers from a sample study of one of the centres. Although the details used are of the Yogashala, similar outline is used by other centres as well.

Understanding Yoga

The word 'yoga' comes from the Sanskrit root '*yuj*' which means to join, to bridge or yoke. It is also translated as union, union of body mind and soul. So yoga is not an end but a means for bridging or uniting the mind and body. 'It also means a 'curriculum' which means a series of studies which a person must undergo to attain certain knowledge. Thus it is a bridge to learning about the True Self.[1] Almost all the Indian spiritual traditions and systems have accepted adopted or incorporated some form or aspects of the spiritual discipline called yoga.[2]

The yoga Upanishads are a group of 20 minor Upanishads related to Yoga. The most prominent among them is the Yogatattva, which mentions about four kinds of yoga. They are; *mantra yoga*, which involves the repetition of mantras or chants, *laya yoga* which focuses on deep concentration and raising the corporal energy known as *kundalini, hatha yoga*, the yoga of force focusing on various postures, breath control and exertion and finally the *raja yoga* which is the classical system of Patanjali focusing on meditation.

The Yoga Sutras traditionally attributed to Patanjali, constitute the basic text of the philosophical system called yoga. The *yoga bhashya* of Vyasa is the earliest commentary on the Yoga Sutras.[3] Raja yoga and Hatha yoga are the two main schools of yoga. Raja yoga is based on the Yoga Sutras of Patanjali while Hatha yoga is the yoga formulated by Gorakshanatha also known as Gorakhnath. He lived around 11th and 12th century. Many legends speak about his yogic powers. It is believed that he and his guru Matsyendranath founded the Nath tradition. However, Gorakhnath is considered as the originator of Hatha Yoga. He has also composed the first book on Laya Yoga and several other books on Yoga. He accepts only six limbs of Yoga (unlike eight limbs in Patanjali yoga). In a nutshell, Raja yoga is concerned with the control of mind while the focus of Hatha yoga is the discipline of body. Hatha yoga enjoys a great appreciation and attraction in the western world. It has a focus on exercise, but it is more than that. The aim of Hatha yoga is to train the body and its internal organs to be in harmony. In fact all forms of yoga aim at producing a state of tranquillity in the subject.[4] The breath-control practiced in all kinds of yogas has the effect on the performer of calming of the nerves and gives a kind of peace at least for a short period. However, it is not the nerves that are calmed but it is the mind that is calmed.

Yoga is defined by Patanjali as 'chittavrittinirodah' which means yoga is the restraint or control (nirodah) of the process or work (vritti) of the mind (chitta). Thus the cessation of the mental process is yoga. The Yoga Sutras describe the method by which this cessation is attained. This method is described in the Yoga Sutras progressively starting from a commitment to an ascetic discipline (tapas). The student then must free himself from all attachment, destroy all desires, and start practice of breath control. The breath control is aimed at reducing the breathing to a minimum which will naturally affect the brain resulting in the reduction of mental activity. Finally the practitioner will concentrate on a luminous point (like repetition of a syllable, image of a deity, ticking of a clock etc.), leading the practitioner to a kind of liberation, 'hibernation' or trance[5].

The Yoga Sutras are concise aphorisms (sutras) which are essential ethical blueprint for living a moral life. The Yoga Sutras are divided into four books with 195 sutras (aphorisms). The first book is 'Of Samadhi' (concentration of mind) which refers to a blissful state into which the student is absorbed. It describes yoga, the nature and the means of attaining the Samadhi. The second book 'Of *Sadhana*' (method) describes two forms of yoga namely the Kriya yoga and the Ashtanga yoga. The third one is 'Of Vibhuti' which means power or manifestation. The combined practice of *dharana dhyana* and *samadhi* bring several siddhis, which the text warns can become an obstacle in the achievement of liberation. The last one is 'Of Kaivalya' which is the final liberation. This section describes the process by which the individual soul achieves liberation.

We can say that the heart of Patanjali's teachings is the eightfold path of yoga. They are (1) *Yama* which is basically the social behaviour, how you treat others and the world around you. These are moral principles. Yama includes five values which are: (a)Ahimsa - non-violence, (b)Satya - truthfulness, honesty, (c) Asteya - non-stealing, coveting (d)Brahmacharya - Continence, chastity, (e)Aparigraha – non-materialism, non-possessiveness. (2)Niyama are basic rules for conduct or positive duties virtuous habits and observances. They are also five in number. (a) *Shaucha* - purity, cleanliness,(b) *Santosha* - contentment, peacefulness,(c) *Tapas* - austerity, (d) *Swadhyaya*- self-study, spiritual study and(e) *Ishwara Pranidhana* -offering of one's life to God.3. Asana (postures practiced in yoga), 4. Pranayama (breath-control), 5. Pratyahara (withdrawal of senses), 6. Dharana (contemplation/ the process of fixing mind on one object), 7. Dhyana (meditation /sustained concentration), and 8. Samadhi (deep absorption/as if mind is devoid of itself).

The third book 'Of Siddhis' (magic powers) discusses the supernatural powers achieved. But the author warns the practitioner not to focus on these powers as it is not the stage of *Kaivalya*. And the last book 'Of Kaivalya' (isolation of the spirit) is the liberation to be achieved. This is the goal of yoga. This book describes the process of liberation and the absolute freedom one achieves by transcending the inner nature. Finally the author also tells the practitioner to serve humankind.

Rishikesh- the World Yoga Capital

Rishikesh is also lately called the yoga capital of the world. There are several registered yoga schools (RYS) offering the Registered Yoga Teacher (RYT) training for 200 hours or 500 hours of classes. It is said that about 90% of Europeans and Americans come to Rishikesh to undergo yoga teacher training and probably to become yoga teachers back in their home country. Yoga might be the most famous aspect among Indian systems popular outside India. Some use yoga as simply exercise, others prefer the meditation techniques or tools for relaxation, and some even claim it as means for their own spirituality. Most of the practitioners are taken up by the initial peace of mind and enjoy the calmness of body and mind. Many people discard the practice after some time. There are hundreds of yoga schools and yoga teachers. Many of them are certified by the United States. Here we introduce only some of the prominent yoga masters and centres.

Some Prominent Yoga Centres and Masters

The whole of Rishikesh is spotted with varieties of yoga centres and yoga teacher training institutes. Most of the ashrams offer good yoga classes. So I do not include the ashrams in this list. Besides the classical ashrams, there are other centres meant primarily for giving yoga courses. I shall present some of that respected yoga here. Defiantly there are several others which are not included in this list.

Yoga Study Centre

One of the genuine yoga teachers is Rudradev Gowda at the Yoga Study Centre, who teaches yoga withoutany fees. A good majority of present teachers at yoga centres in Rishikesh are his disciples. Gowda follows the tradition of his famous guru B.K.S

Iyengar. His centre is situated at the Ganga Vihar, Koyal Ghati. Before starting his own centre, he had been teaching yoga at Sivananda Ashram for almost ten years. He has been teaching yoga in Rishikesh for more than 25 years. He is a real Master of Yoga who continues to learn with the attitude of a student. He lives a life of asceticism and is devoted to practicing what he teaches.

He is much disciplined and wants his students to be fully committed when learning yoga. This centre conducts daily yoga classes as well as some intensive short period yoga courses.

Omkarananda Patanjala Yoga Centre

Another disciple of B.K.S Iyengar, Usha Devi teaches yoga at the Patanjali Yoga centre established in the Omkarananda Ganga Sadan. Usha Devi moved to her adopted home India in 1985. This yoga centre was established in 1993. Usha Devi studied yoga from 1993 and continues to learn. She had met with two road accidents and recovered fully and continues to teach and practice yoga. She is very precise, disciplined, and strict in her lessons. She wants her students to take the classes seriously. We can say that she is one of the most prominent yoga teachers at Rishikesh.

Jeevanmoksha Yoga Gurukul

Acharya Vinay is a good yoga teacher at the Jeevanmoksha yoga gurukul. He started to study yoga from his father at an early age. He was officially initiated into yoga by Guru Rudranath who follows the Nath tradition. He also got initiated into the Sri Vidya tradition of Tantra. He holds a master's degree in Yogic science and offers regular classes. This centre has regular classes on yoga as well as retreats and courses on yoga for varying days. This rather small Gurukul is situated in Tapovan.

Rishikesh Yog Peeth

It is in Rishikesh Yog Peeth that Roshan Singh teaches Ashtanga and Hatha yoga. He is a good yoga teacher and he takes a lead in conducting yoga courses. This centre has a variety of courses and could be considered as one of the best yoga schools presently in Rishikesh. This centre offers yoga teacher training and yoga courses regularly. This centre is situated at the Krishna Cottage of Swarg Ashram.

Tattavaa Yoga Shala

Yogi Kamal Singh is the senior yoga teacher trainer at Tattavaa Yoga Centre. He is known for his dynamic yoga classes. He focuses on the physical aspect of yoga and makes the students work more on their body. This centre also offers several kinds of yoga teacher training and courses. It is situated near Ram jhula at Swarg ashram premises.

Rishikesh Yogis Yogashala

A group of yoga masters of Rishikesh Yogis Yogashala, including Sushant and Uttam offer world-class yoga and meditation courses in Tapovan. Guru Sushant is an alumnus of the famous Bihar school of Yoga. He had been a yoga teacher at several institutes before the starting of Yogis Yogashala. They also travel around the world especially to the United States, Russia, Europe, and Thailand to teach yoga and conduct yoga retreats. However, they feel most at home in Rishikesh. They specialize in unique and custom retreats for groups.

A Detailed Study of a Yoga Centre

Let us now take up one of the centres of Yoga and explore how a Yoga centre functions and what are the subjects taught. We shall also deal with their schedule and programmes. We shall take up one centre and understand their program to get a clearer picture. Most of the good Yoga centres offer something similar.

General Outline of Courses

Concerning the yoga teacher trainings the centres have separate 100, 200, 300- or 500-hours teacher trainings. Since Yoga is vast and the trainings are meant for teachers the topics and the syllabus are divided into several sub-divisions. Most centres offer *Kundalini* yoga teacher trainings and *Ashtanga Vinyasa* yoga teacher trainings (sometimes catering to only one language group such as Spanish or French). Depending on the need and demand many centres also offer *Ashtanaga Vinyasa* yoga teacher trainings and *Hatha Vinyasa* yoga teacher trainings.

Besides these teacher trainings, the centres often arrange yoga retreats for small or big groups. These retreats are also sub-divided into *Kriya* yoga and *kundalini kriya* yoga retreats. The duration of these retreats are normally limited to 10 days, 15 days or even one month.The duration of these retreats are normally limited to 10 days, 15 days or even one month.

The Daily Schedule

The spiritual masters of ancient times have taught the Indians about the importance of rising early. They say that rising at what is called the *Brahmamuhurta*, which means the auspicious time of Brahma, which is roughly calculated between 4 to 6 am., helps the individuals to grow in the good qualities (sattva guna) and to destroy the negativities (tamas guna). They teach us that our lives are inter-connected to the nature, especially to the Sun. Therefore, they advocate rising early to be ready to welcome the rising sun in the early morning (and perform the *suryanamaskar* i.e. the salutations to the sun).

The schedule of the yoga centres are made according to this rhythm of the nature. The participants are expected rise early and be ready for a cup of green tea normally around 06.00 to 06.30 am. It is followed by silent meditation in groups around 07.00. This is mostly done as a silent relaxed sitting. This brief session prepares the participants to become aware of one's inner self. This is followed by guided chanting of mantra and pranayama meditation which lasts for one hour. First, the participants are taught what a mantra is and how it is to be recited. They are also guided in the practical exercise of pranayama giving individual attention. Guidance is given about the meaning, procedure, and its benefits. Step by step guidance with personal attention enables the students to learn mantra and pranayama meditation.

The theory cum practice session of yoga is followed normally until 09.30. It is called the alignment and adjustment session. What is done here is the teaching of the basics of yoga, starting with lessons on yoga posture that too dividing them into sub postures. Each posture is explained, and the right alignment of the body is taught thoroughly. While practicing yoga, injuries to the body must be avoided. Therefore at each pose, how the body must be aligned and how the body rhythm and the natural movements of each body part according to the anatomy of the body is taught with care and attention. This step by step exercise with theory helps in the aligning the body properly when yoga is practiced in the advanced stage. This session is followed by breakfast which is pure vegetarian. In fact the whole meal always is yogic and vegetarian.

The one-hour session normally around 10.30 is called yoga theory session which is devoted to the teaching of Philosophy, Anatomy, and the Psychology of Yoga. This theoretical session is engaged by experts in each field. For example, the yoga anatomy deals with the functions of each bone, muscle, gland or body part and its importance, their role and relevance in the yoga practice and in the well-being of the human body. Similarly the functioning of mental organs is also particularly important in yoga. The session also discusses the relevant and right attitude for yoga. There is also a well-developed philosophical system of Yoga. The basic vision and basics of yoga philosophy is taught in these sessions.

The next session from 11.30 or so until lunch is meant for guided meditation. This session teaches the participants much needed concentration techniques, the art of withdrawal of senses from sense objects and the step by step progress in meditation. At 13.00 hours everyone gathers for lunch and relaxation for one hour. Thereafter a free time is given to internalize the classes, and to do personal works.

Tea is served between 15.00 to 15.30 hours, which is followed by karma yoga for 45 minutes. This teaches the participants the importance of karma and how any work even mundane jobs can be made use of as a spiritual means.

At 16.30 hours the Theory session II on Philosophy and teaching methodology is resumed. Here the traditional Indian yoga philosophy is given focus. The Vedanta philosophy, the Samkhya and Yoga philosophy and the teaching methodology is discussed in this session. After a brief break they gather again at 17.45 for the traditional Hatha Vinyasa Yoga experiential class. It is conducted in a continuous flow. It is also a theme-based session. For example one day it might be focused on the lower back or on shoulder or neck etc. This session is followed by dinner at 19.00 hours. Dinner and the relaxation time last until 20.15 hours. The centres normally require the participants to remain within the premises and participate in the complete schedule. Usually the participants are advised to put off the light by 22.00 hours to get a good night's sleep to keep them fresh for the next day morning. Keeping silence and going to bed early are important as silence helps one to internalize the whole day's program and enough rest and sleep keeps one fresh to rise early the next day.

Special Programs and Activities

Once a week there is cleaning practice called the *shat kriya*. It is the exercise of cleaning the parts of body such as nails, nostrils, lungs, stomach etc. There are also some other external activities arranged for the students. The participants are given an opportunity to explore the important city sites by arranging periodic tours and visits. They are normally taken to the hills of Kujapuri temple outside the city for a sunrise meditation. They are also taken out to participate in the Ganga *aarti* preferably at Paramarth Niketan together with all other pilgrims and devotees. A walking tour of Sivananda Ashram and a visit to Vashist gufa (cave) is also arranged. If the students are interested an outing is arranged to the beautiful Patna waterfall and a walking tour of Rishikesh town is also arranged.

The Methodology of the Program

At the yoga centres, the ashram lifestyle is followed with a focus on disciple and self-awareness. The teachers or masters focus on giving personal attention, hence the limited number for each training. They give opportunity for the students to lead the yoga exercises and classes in animated sessions to find out if the students have learned the steps well. The classes are given by committed experts in the field who are properly qualified. For them, the teaching of yoga is not a job but a *sadhana* (spiritual means) and so what they do is undertaken with commitment and devotion. The team of masters accompany the participants full time. They look up to the participants as their honoured guests and not as students.

Endnotes

[1] Aubrey Menen, *The Mystics*, New York, The Dial Press, 1974, p101.

[2] Shrinavas Tilak, *Religion and Aging in Indian Tradition,* New York, State University of New York Press, 1989, p.12.

[3] Vacaspati Mishra's *Tattvavaisaradi* seeks to throw light upon and explain both the Yog Sutra and yoga bhashya.

[4] Aubrey Menen, *The Mystics*, New York, The Dial Press, 1974, p.110.

[5] Fernando Tola & Carmen Dragonetti, *The Yogasutras of Patanjali: On Concentration of mind,* translated by K. D. Prithipaul, (Delhi, Motilal Banarsidas Publishers, 1987), p.xiii.

An Introduction to Hinduism

Understanding Hinduism requires the basic knowledge and familiarity with the framework and worldview of Hinduism. The rituals, the spirituality (next chapter) and the general Hindu mind can better be understood by studying the Hindu framework. If you want to know why the Hindus do what they do, why do they not go regularly to temple, or why do they take spiritual life seriously, or why do they become monks etc., then you need to grasp the basic Hindu framework. Therefore one can understand Hinduism and Hindu spirituality in a better way if they are comprehended within the Hindu framework or the Hindu worldview.

The Hindu Framework

Hinduism cannot be reduced to a religion but is an amalgamation Hinduism cannot be reduced to a religion but is an amalgamation of cultures, religions and ethics linked coherently together in a framework[1]. In general, we could perceive a cyclic worldview in Hinduism. In this section we shall give a brief outline of the Hindu world view. We do not treat the whole of Hindu worldview but limit ourselves only to the spiritual aspects. First, we shall present a short exposition of the Hindu understanding of God, cosmos and human beings that are the basis and the basics of any worldview. Thereafter we shall present the Hindu spiritual framework. The goal of the spiritual life and methods, or rather, the paths taken by the Hindus in reaching their target, becomes the focus of our investigation. Thereafter, the Hindu temple worship together with the urban and rural spiritual practices will be explored to unearth the framework behind these spiritual practices.

The Concept of God[2]

An examination of the Vedic texts gives us the idea that there were different gods like Indra, Agni, Varun and others who were at different times at the centre of the Vedic religion[3]. The Epic and Puranic texts exalt new deities and slowly marginalized the Vedic deities. What we find here is the emergence of Shaiva (Saiva), Vaishnava (Vaisnava) and Shakta (Sakta) deities. Unlike the Vedic deities, these three come to prominence, stay for long time, and continue to play a central role in the lives of majority of Hindus. Brahma is also occasionally cited as part of the *trimurti* (trinity), or three forms of a supreme divinity Brahm, in which Brahma is the creator, Vishnu is the preserver and Shiva is the destroyer. However, Shiva and Vishnu come to prominence. Only a few temples in India offer worship to Brahma and his worship has become virtually extinct[4]. Shiva becomes the important figure as the One God and the Lord for many millions of Hindus. Shiva the God responsible for destruction stands out as the 'great God' among all the deities of the Hindu religion[5]. The phallic emblem the linga as symbol of the creative power of Shiva is the most widely venerated cult-object in Shiva worship[6]. At the same time Vishnu grows in stature and through his incarnations incorporates other deities such as Rama and Krishna who have their own cults[7]. Vishnu tradition has the greatest books of Indian literature of which Ramayana and Mahabharata are prominent ones. This god takes several manifestations and is highly active in the lives of people through numerous incarnations of various degrees. Among the incarnations, Rama and Krishna enjoy particular favour and an immense literature, stories and myths have grown around them[8]. The Shiva mythologies associate Ganesha (the elephant-headed deity) with Shiva's family while Hanuman (the deity in the form of monkey) is associated with Rama and thus incorporated into the Vishnu worship[9]. "The genealogies and family trees of the main deities so frequent in the Puranas are attempts, not always successful, to coordinate the various popular deities and to make them appear, if not as manifestations of the one God, then at least as his children or servants"[10]. Goddesses assume the role of the Supreme Being in Shaktism tradition. It is in Tantras that the goddesses come to occupy the supreme place. Shakti means "power" personified in the Goddess, the Divine Mother to whom are ascribed all the functions of Vishnu and Shiva. The worship of mother goddesses is especially important even today. Parvati, Kali and Durga have a great following among the Hindus. Although historically, the development of Shaktism, as an organized form of religion with its own theology came after the development of Shaivism and Vaishnavism, today almost all schools of Hinduism have strong elements of Shaktism blended with their teaching[11].

In the Upanishads Brahman becomes the term around which the loftiest religious speculation has revolved for thousands of years and it is still the term used to designate the Supreme Being[12]. The speculative philosophy of the Upanishads developed in the subsequent centuries into what is known as the *Vedanta* philosophy[13]. The *Vedanta* focuses on the study and understanding of the Upanishads. There are five schools of Vedanta, of which three namely *Advaita* (non-duality), the *Vishistadvaita* (qualified non-duality) and the *Dvaita* (duality) are important. The other two are schools of Vallabha and Nimbarka. They speak of the relationship between the absolute supreme Brahman and the individual *atma* (soul). This *Vedanta* school of thought has come down to the present day and gives us rather a coherent concept of God. We shall discuss the vision of God as seen in the first three schools.

According to the *Advaita* School of Shankara (traditionally 788-820), there is only one thing that is absolutely real, and that is Brahman. It teaches that Brahman is the only thing in existence and with Brahman the cosmic and the individual souls are one[14]. This Brahman is indivisible and *nirguna* i.e. without attributes[15]. "This term denotes a non-dual pure consciousness which pervades the universe and yet remains outside of it".[16] This Brahman cannot be the object of worship or prayer, and no relationship whatsoever can be established with it[17]. By means of its own inscrutable power called *maya* (illusion) the unconditioned Brahman, manifests itself as the conditioned Brahman (*saguna* Brahman*)* endowed with attributes - the personal God. The God conceived through the mind as having divine qualities is this personal God, *saguna* Brahman or Ishwara[18].

The *Vishistadvaita* of Ramanuja (1056-1137) upholds that there is only one Absolute Reality and that is Brahman, but it is qualified because according to him it is meaningless to comprehend, relate or to speak about a *nirguna* Brahman. Therefore, he says that *maya* is real and Brahman is *saguna* and is Ishwara or possessing qualities[19]. The soul or *atman* is not identical with Brahman, but is the aspect of Brahman, wholly depended upon him. The world for him is real and creation, preservation and destruction are the activities of Brahman[20].

The *Dvaita* of Madhva (1238-1317) postulates the existence of three types of entities namely Brahman (Ishwar), soul (*jivatma*) and matter (*prakrti*). However, he speaks of God who creates the universe as the independent reality while the universe that is created by God has a dependent existence. Madhva emphasizes on the absolute independence and the unutterable majesty of Brahman and stresses upon the two aspects of divinity namely the perfection of being and freedom from all limitations[21]. The souls are limited by both space and attributes and possess only temporal pervasion in the sense of existing at all times[22]. The souls and the matter are dependent on Brahman for existence, but Brahman is totally independent. Madhva says that the soul is placed at the centre of the triple categories of Ishwar-*jivatma-prakṛti*. Therefore, the soul can get involved in the meshes of *sansara* or bondage when the soul leans towards the matter. The soul gets liberated if he leans to the other side. Madhva considers God as *saguna* and as personal and he identifies the Brahman of the *Vedanta* with Vishnu[23]. Thus, Vishnu is not just one deity but the supreme One, the object of worship, and all other gods are subordinated to Him.

Normally, the ordinary people believe that God is one in all the manifestations, and all the manifestations are of God himself. "They may not be able to figure out in theological terms how the many gods and the One God hang together and they may not be sure about the hierarchy among the many manifestations, but they know that ultimately there is only One and that the many somehow merge into the One"[24]. Therefore, they accept the extended powers of God working in nature and name it accordingly. Because of this kind of faith when some people claim to be the incarnation of Vishnu, people in general accept such claims. Hindu theology has many ways of explaining the unity of Brahman in the diversity of deities, meeting the different needs of the people and incorporating the local traditions and specific revelations.

The Vision of Cosmos

The origin of the visible world is explained in Hindu mythology in various ways[25]. The Vedas have two important descriptions in *Purusha Sukta* and *nasadiya sukta*. The earth is described in *Purusha Sukta* as emerging from the thousand-headed, thousand-eyed, and thousand-footed *purusha* (the cosmic being) a kind of primeval giant to whom gods themselves sacrifice. He emanated a female creative principle called *viraj* and from this he is reborn, and then his parts became the world. The moon came from his spirit, the sun from his eyes, the heavens from his skull. From his mouth the *Brahmins* emerged, while from his arms, thighs and feet came the other *varnas* (castes)[26]. The *nasadiya sukta*[27] is a cosmology hymn that briefly describes the chaos that preceded creation, as there was neither existence nor non-existence, no sky, no earth, there was neither death nor immortality. But there was only the Breath which breathed breathlessly. This breath desired to create and there was creation.

The Hindu cosmology is cyclical[28]. In general, Hindus consider both the time and the creation as in a repetitive cyclical move. The created world does not have a singular history, "the universe has come into being several times and gone out of existence several times and this process has been going on from beginningless time and will go on forever"[29]. God the Brahma brings the cosmos as we have mentioned earlier, into existence and He, as Vishnu, sustains it and as Shiva, He is the destroyer of this universe. It is not an act done finally. We can speak neither of a creation nor of a real destruction, but only a manifestation on the one hand and dissolution on the other[30].

A clear description of the Hindu cosmos with its cyclical creation scheme of time subdivided into *yugas* (an era or an age), *manvantaras* (age of manu, i.e. manu+*antara*=*manvantara*), and so on, as well as its spatial layout of islands and concentric oceans, are found in the *puranic* writings[31]. There are four *yugas* called *Krita* or *Satya*, *Treta*, *Dvapara*, and *Kali*. "The basic cycle is the *kalpa*, a day of Brahma which is equal to 4320 million earthly years. His night is of equal length. Three hundred and sixty such days and nights constitute a year of Brahma and his life lasts for 100 such years. The largest cycle is therefore 311,040,000 million years long, after which the whole universe returns to the ineffable world spirit, until another creator god is evolved"[32].

According to the general Hindu understanding the universe is shaped like an egg called *Brahmanda* or the egg of Brahma. Though there are some variations in the descriptions of these worlds, it is in general called as *tri-loka* i.e. triple world system, namely the world of heavens, the world of human beings and the underworld[33]. It is different from the Christian understanding of heaven, earth and hell. According to Hinduism, this cosmos has 21 zones, 6 above the earth called the heavens, seven below the earth called the *patal* or the nether earth, below it there are 7 zones called the *narak* or hell. The six heavens are of an increasing beatitude. The *patal* is the abode of *nagas* and other mythical beings but not an unpleasant place, whereas, the *narak* is conceived as having an existence of increasing misery and are inhabited by souls in torment[34].

The Upanishads present the world on the one hand as coming from Brahman, and on the other hand as Brahman. "As the hair and nails grow on a living person, as the threads come out of a spider, as sparks fly from a burning fire, as melodies issue from a flute, or waves rise on the ocean, so also the universe came from Brahman"[35]. According to Brihadaranyaka Upanishad, in the beginning there was only the Supreme Being. He looked around and saw nothing beside himself. He divided himself into two: husband and wife. Thus human beings were created. She turned into a cow and he became a bull. She turned into a mare, he became a stallion. And thus various kinds of animals came into existence[36].

Vedanta philosophy, especially for Shankara and Ramanuja the visible world has its origin in Brahman, the Absolute[37]. For Shankara the world is *maya* (illusion) or appearance, and for Ramanuja, it is the body of God, sharing some of the qualities of God[38]. Many people share the idea that temporal goods or the world is *maya* or delusionary, but it is from God, therefore it has the presence of divinity. For Madhva, the matter (*prakrti*) and souls (*jivatman*) have their own reality and existence but are eternally depended on Brahman. This Brahman takes on a personal role and controls the universe. Madhva speaks of five fundamental, eternal, and real differences that exists, namely between individual soul (*jiva*) and God (Brahman/Vishnu), between matter (*prakrti*) and Brahman, between matter and souls, among souls (*jivatman*) and among various types of matter. Therefore, one of the important features of this world is that it is characterized by duality. The opposites of *dharma* and *adharma*, good and evil, hot, and cold, gods and demons co-exist in this world[39].

The Vision of Human Beings

According to the Hindu thinking, the human being possesses three bodies and a spirit called *jiva* or atma. The three bodies are the gross physical body, the subtle body, and the causal body[40]. The *atma* is that element in the human being, which is not subject to change, and is the core of one's being. This can exist without bodies, while the bodies cannot exist without the *atma*[41].

One's spiritual identity is that of an individual *jiva* or *atma*. This *atma* is a spark of God[42]. At the same time, similar sparks of God are seen in all the external things like rivers, trees, human beings, animals, oceans, stars, sun, moon, mountains and even in land. Everything is seen as an extension of God and so they are divine. This *atma* is neither born nor dies even when the body is dead. In Bhagavad Gita this process is compared to the way a person puts on new garments after giving up old ones, the *atma* takes up new material body after giving up the old ones[43]. Therefore, one person carries with him or her the fruits of his/her action from one life to the next. Those that lead a wicked life take birth as subhuman beings. Those who fulfilled their moral duties, and sought the results of their action, go to the plane of moon (lesser heaven) and reap their fruits of actions, and are reborn as human beings. And those who lead an intense spiritual life on earth, go to the *brahmaloka* (the world of Brahma/highest heaven) and some obtain liberation and some return to the earth[44].

Vedanta describes human beings as a 5-layered entity, one layer upon another like the sheaths of an onion[45]. The outermost layer refers to the physical body and is termed as *annamayatman* (the corporal layer), the second is the *pranamayatman* (the biological layer) while the third is the *manomayatman* (the psychological layer). The fourth inner layer is called the *vijnanamayatman* (the intellectual layer) while *anandamayatman* (pure bliss) is the fifth and innermost layer of the *jiva*. Shankara considers reality as Brahman and so the individual reality is only *maya*. It has its implications for spiritual life, which we shall deal with below. Ramanuja believes that the *jiva* is eternal and is of the same substance as that of Brahman[46]. *Jiva* is a particle of which God is the whole. The individual souls are distinct from each other and are viewed as the body of Brahman. It sprung from Brahman and will enjoy its separate existence. Madhva teaches that the distinction between Brahman and soul is real but the individual souls depend on Brahman. The *jivas* are innumerable and they are eternal and undergo suffering because of the connection with material body.

Hindu Scriptures

In general the Hindu scriptures are classified into two broad divisions. First is called *shruti* which means that which is heard, and the second is called *smriti* which means that which is remembered.

Shruti

Shruti may be characterized as the revelatory part of the Hindu scriptures[47]. They are considered as revealed by God himself and canonical in nature. These comprise the central canon of Hinduism. The Shrutis are believed to be eternal and *apauruseya* which means having no human author but transmitted by sages (rishis). The Shrutis include the four Vedas (Rig, Sama, Yajur, Atharva), the Brahmanas (commentaries on rituals, ceremonies and sacrifices), the Aranyakas (texts on rituals, ceremonies, sacrifices and symbolic-sacrifices), and the Upanishads (texts discussing meditation, philosophy and spiritual knowledge). Some scholars add a fifth category - the Upasanas (worship) as well to this section.

The Vedas are a large body of Hindu texts originating in ancient India, completed before about 800 BCE. Composed in Vedic Sanskrit hymns, the texts constitute the oldest layer of Sanskrit literature and the oldest scriptures of Hinduism. The Brahmanas are a collection of ancient texts with commentaries on the hymns of the four Vedas and explanation of sacrifices. They are descriptions of the different types of sacrifices and rituals. The Aryankas, which means the forest treatise, are the continuation of Brahmanas and the beginning of Upanishads. These books are more philosophical in nature than ritualistic. The Upanishads are commonly referred to as Vedanta. They primarily discuss philosophy, meditation, and the nature of God. They form the core spiritual thought of Vedantic Hinduism. The teachings of the Upanishads, and those of the Bhagavat Gita, form the basis of the Vedanta philosophy.

Smriti

Smritis are attributed to an author. Their function is to interpret, substantiate and sublimate the Shruti books.[48] Smritis are codes of conduct for both social and private life, and expiation (prayschita). Under Smriti comes the **Vedangas**, which provide the necessary tools to interpret the Vedic word correctly and to perform the Vedic rituals in the correct manner and time, the **Itihasas** (epics) among which Ramayana and Mahabharata are well-known, the **Agamas**, the **Darshanas**, **Dharmashastras** and the **Puranas**. Among all these the Puranas need a small description.

Puranic tradition is too vast to define; the very sources from which it draws its beliefs and practices are so numerous and so heterogeneous that any attempt to come to general conclusions is doomed to failure. There are 18 important and larger ones called Maha Puranas and 18 smaller called Upa Puranas. Because of their mythological and religious character, many western scholars originally bypassed them. But now more serious study is being done on them.

The kind of Hinduism articulated in Puranas makes much of individual revelations of deities in dreams and visions, gives great importance to personalities considered manifestations of a deity, and is as important for the economy as for spirituality in India. Often it is said, Shruti and Smriti are two eyes of Dharma but Purana is its heart.

It is important to note that the religion represented by the Puranas is the one that makes Hinduism what it is. I would call it as the daily Bible of Hinduism. The Puranas deal with the creation of the universe and its dissolutions at the end times. They vividly describe cycle and age of the worlds, the genealogies of the sages, several stories of the salvific deeds of God and many other subjects including codes of ethics and the four aims of life. They also deal with the several religious observances, places of pilgrimage, rituals and descriptions of heavens and hells. They are inexhaustible storehouse of all kinds of information for anyone interested in Hinduism.

They are explicitly sectarian and represent the scriptures of Vainavism, Shaivism and Shaktism. They insist on exclusively worshiping the deity which they make the centre of presentation and attribute salvific effects only to their own sectarian practices. They reflect the attitudes of present-day Hindus and continue to mould their minds more than any other source. Widely available, publicly read, they promise instant and rich rewards for reading and preserving them and make it easy for the adherents to embark on the way to bliss and salvation.

However, besides the Puranas, we also must consider the Itihasas namely Mahabharata and Ramayana, and in a special way the Gita which is treated as the epitome of Hindu faith on which innumerable lectures, literature, interpretations and discourses are given. These together can be considered as the main source of Hinduism as practiced today by millions of Hindus.

Endnotes

[1] Hinduism has neither single founder nor one religious leader. It has neither single religious symbol nor single holy place.

[2] For a detailed description of the Hindu vision of God, See, Kuttiyanikkal C.J., *Khrist Bhakta Movement; A Model for an Indian Church?*,Munster/ London, LiT Verlag, 2014, pp194-196.

[3] K.K. Klostermaier, *A Survey of Hinduism*, New York, State University of New York Press, 1989, p. 128.

[4] *Ibid.*, p. 133. The most important temple of Brahma is the Pushkar Temple in Rajasthan.

[5] Asharose, 'Shiva', in V. MATAJI (ed.), *Shabda Shakti Sangam*, Rishikesh, Jeevan-dhara Sadhana Kutir, 1995, p. 37. The followers of Shiv are called *Saivites*. One should not associate destruction as negative but at the appointed time he does consummation or transformation.

[6] P. Fallon, 'The Gods of Hinduism', in R. Antoine, et al, (eds.), *Religious Hinduism. A Presentation and Appraisal,* Allahabad, St. Paul Publications, 1968, p. 85.

[7] H. Rodrigues, *Introducing Hinduism*, New York/London, Routledge, 2006, p. 190.

[8] K.K. Klostermaier, *A Survey of Hinduism*, New York, State University of New York Press, 1989, p. 139.

[9] There are also plenty of temples in honour of Hanuman and GaGes.

[10] Klostermaier, *A Survey of Hinduism*, p. 142.

[11] *Ibid.*, p. 275.

[12] *Ibid.*, p. 132.

[13] Rodrigues, *Introducing Hinduism*, New York/ London, Routledge, 2006, p. 249.

[14] S. Cave, *Redemption. Hindu and Christian*, London, Oxford University Press, 1919, p. 17.

[15] Rodrigues, *Introducing Hinduism*, p. 250.

[16] S. Nikhilananda, *Hinduism. Its Meaning for the Liberation of the Spirit*, London, George Allen & Unwin Ltd, 1958, p. 29.

[17] *Ibid.*, p. 35.

[18] S. Nityesthananda, 'The Concept of God in Hinduism', in V. Mataji (ed.), *Shabda Shakti Sangam*, p. 21.

[19] Rodrigues, *Introducing Hinduism*, p. 252.

[20] Nikhilananda, *Hinduism*, p. 36.

[21] B.N.K. Sharma, *Philisophy of Sri Madhavcarya*, Delhi, Motilal Banarsidas, 1986, pp. 323-329.

[22] *Ibid.*, p. 329

[23] Rodrigues, *Introducing Hinduism*, p. 253.

[24] Klostermaier, *A Survey of Hinduism*, p. 144.

[25] Besides what we present here the myth of *HiraGyagarbha* from Rig Veda is also important.

[26] A. Michaels, *Hinduism. Past and Present*, trans. Barbara Harshav, Princeton, Princeton University Press, 1998, p. 286.

[27] Rig Veda, 10.129

[28] In Western worldview, the cosmos comes into existence once and goes out once and for all. But In Hinduism, everything is cyclical, and has no beginning and end, but goes on eternally.

[29] A. Sharma, *Classical Hindu Thought. An Introduction*, Oxford, Oxford University Press, 2000, pp. 5-6.

[30] It is the duty of Vishnu to ensure that the dissolution does not happen prematurely. Therefore he takes *avatars* to rectify or bring back the normalcy in case of defect. Up to now he has taken 9 *avataras* namely as a fish, tortoise, boar, a man-lion, dwarf, Parasuram, Rama, K[ishna and Buddha. And one more is to come at the end of this age, and then Shiva would put an end to this cycle and then emerges the next one. See for details A.L. Basham, *The Wonder that was India*, London, Sidwick & Jackson, 1968, Reprint,p. 6.

[31] Rodrigues, *Introducing Hinduism*, p. 189.

[32] Basham, *The Wonder that was India*, p. 323.

[33] Rodrigues, *Introducing Hinduism*, p. 49.

[34] Basham, *The Wonder that was India*, p. 490.

[35] Nikhilananda, *Hinduism*, pp. 40-41.

[36] Klostermaier, *A Survey of Hinduism*, p. 111.

[37] *Ibid.* p. 123.

[38] *Ibid.*

[39] *Ibid.*

[40] A. Sharma, *Classical Hindu Thought. An Introduction*, Oxford, Oxford University Press, 2000, p. 9.

[41] *Ibid.* In the rebirth, the subtle body and causal body (not physical) together with *atman* migrate.

[42] As the unconditioned Brahman, in association with *maya* manifests itself as conditioned Brahman, so also in association with the same *maya*, it becomes the individual soul. Under the control of *maya* the individual soul forgets its real nature, while the conditioned Brahman keeps the *maya* under his control. See for details Nikhilananda, *Hinduism*, pp. 49-50.

[43] *The Bhagavat Gita*, 2. 22.

[44] Therefore the view of an individual as born into a higher or lower caste is merited by the conduct in a prior life. For details see, M. Weber, *The Religion of India*, Illinois, The Free Press, 1960, p. 121.

[45] E.S. Palispis, *Introduction to Values Education*, Quezon City, Rex Book Store, 1995, pp. 47-48.

[46] Ramanuja speaks about three types of souls namely the *nitya* (eternal, the *mukta* (free) and the *baddha* (bound).

[47] A.Thottakara, *Indian Spirituality*, Bangalore, Dharmaram

Chapter - 7

An Introduction to Hindu Spirituality

The Aim of Spirituality

Although Hindu spirituality speaks about Moksha to refer to various forms of emancipation, enlightenment, liberation and release, it is different from the Semitic understanding of salvation. It is true that for Hindus Moksha is a central concept and one of the four aims of life, but it is understood rather as a process of Divine Realization. This must be understood against the basic Hindu concept of human being's present condition not as in sin but as in ignorance. Therefore spirituality is aimed at removing darkness or ignorance of the soul. In Hinduism it is not sin, but ignorance is the greatest obstacle to salvation or what is called enlightenment. Because of ignorance one is caught up in *samsara* which means the cycle of births and deaths. Therefore the spiritual pursuit is to free the soul from this cycle. Hence the question which path or *marga* should I choose to free my soul from this *samsara*[1].

One can understand Hinduism and Hindu spirituality in a better way if they are comprehended within the Hindu framework or the Hindu worldview (the previous chapter). The spiritual life for most of the Hindus today is closely related to the faith in *karma* theory[2]. The accumulated sum of good or bad is called *karma*.This means that human actions are binding on the individual soul. Intricately linked is the faith in the transmigration of soul, which means that the soul enters another body after death. The actions of an individual in the previous life determine the status of the present life. The deeds of present life decide the condition of next life. Thus human life is a cycle of births, deaths, and rebirths. Liberation called *moksha,* happens finally when the soul gets out of this cycle or *samsara*. The spiritual pursuit is to save the soul from this cycle. Thus attainment of *moksha* is considered as the supreme goal or aim of spiritual life[3].

Sacrificial Hinduism

Ancient Hindu spirituality was centred on *yajna* or sacrifice. Historically, in the ancient *Vedic* times there was a lot of stress on *yajna* (sacrifice). For the ancient Hindus nothing was possible without *yajna* and all was attainable through *yajna*[4]. It was performed by qualified priests and in the prescribed form. Oblations were poured into the fire as a means of offering them to the gods. The aim of the performance was often gaining certain results in life, mostly material results[5]. Sacrifices were performed for gaining all sorts of worldly goods and they were also considered great remedies for all the ills of life[6]. Performing a sacrifice required money, time, and experts. Important and big sacrifices were carried out only by the ruling class. For the sacrifice, the rituals had to be done in the prescribed manner and by prescribed priests/Brahmins. The focus was on performing the sacrifice in the correct form.

Contemplative Hinduism

Performing sacrifice was not possible for all. Mostly it became mere ritualism and devoid of any personal touch. Many times the performer was paid, and the owner just became a passive participant. It was long also, expensive and limited only to the higher varnas and rich people. So there emerged the contemplative spirituality with the *Upanishadic* period. During this period, ritualism was considered as inferior, although the *yajna* tradition continued to exist on one side, and *upasana* (contemplation) takes the centre stage. "Contemplation became the dominant mode of spiritual life for Hindus following the decline of *Vedic* culture"[7]. The *Upanishadic* age is the age of real knowledge of the Self, and all great scholars of this age were interested in self-realization, through the knowledge of identity between the *atma* and the Brahman[8].

Devotional Hinduism

The emergence of the *bhakti* tradition marked the devotion to a personal God. The *bhakti* tradition which started in southern India spread to central and northern India with the emergence of several poet saints[9]. The *bhakti* tradition got a boost with the philosophical teachings of Ramanuja and Madhva. According to Ramanuja the central act of *bhakti* is self-surrender. According to Madhva, liberation is ultimately the result of God's grace (*prasada*).

The Three Prominent Spiritual Paths

In general there are several spiritual paths in Hinduism. Historically, the Mimamsa School had laid great stress on rituals, or Karma-Kanda. According to the (purva) Mimamsa school, Karma, or ritual is the only means in the Veda. Worship and Knowledge are only accessories to Karma. However, according to the Vedanta, Knowledge is the foremost thing, and ritual and worship are accessories. On the other hand, according to the *Bhakti* school the final emancipation can be obtained only through *Bhakti* and the grace of the Lord. The grace of the Lord comes through devotion and Prapatti or absolute self-surrender. Karma and Jnana are means to *Bhakti*. The other paths are mostly a combination of these or developed from these basic paths.

The Bhagavad Gita articulates these spiritual paths clearly and gives us a clearer understanding of each of these paths. Although divided into eighteen chapters, each of which is called a teaching on a particular *yoga* or discipline, its teachings are conventionally grouped into the above mentioned three major approaches to liberation[10]. An individual may choose any of these *margas*. But many times people follow a mixture of the paths since the practice of one *marga* does not exclude the others. The *jnana marga* requires study and meditation and is largely preferred by the intellectual elite, and the *karma marga* is preferred by those who are supposed to continue to remain in the society and has the advantage of being practical[11]. The *bhakti marga* has a universal appeal. It promises salvation and heaven to all the castes, women, and children. Therefore *bhakti marga* has greater following and appreciation among the ordinary people.

A better comprehension of the Hindu spiritual framework is possible by grasping the thinking that is lying at the foundation of these *margas*. In India, renunciation of the world for attaining *moksha* was considered the preferred spiritual path for attaining liberation, but it was not possible for all the people to renounce the world. The *karma marga* gives an option for those people who want to stay in the world, or those who are forced to stay in the world, because it combines action and renunciation. This path consists in performing the duties of one's station in life with a spirit of detachment[12]. The duty of one person depends on his *ashrama* (stage of life) and *varna*[13]. According to this *marga* the action is not given up, but the fruit of the action is given up. It is explained in Bhagavad Gita as, "set thy heart upon work, but never on its reward. Work thou not for a reward; but never shall thou cease to do thy work"[14]. The aim of *karma marga* is to keep the *atma* free from the fruit of the actions - both good and bad actions. For every action, there is resultant fruit, and the *atma* must bear the fruit. If action is good, then a good or higher life will be followed, while if action is bad, then, a lower life. In both cases one is caught up in *samsara* (the repeating cycle of birth, life death and rebirth). By giving up the fruits of the actions one gets rid of the cycle.

The *jnana marga* is directed towards the *nirguna* Brahman and it aims at the attainment of God realization, which is identifying the *atma* (individual soul) with the *paramatman* (Supreme Being). The idea behind this path is the realization that what is real is the Brahman and all else is *maya*. The individual soul is none other than the universal soul[15]. Through knowledge one must come to this realization, then there is no need for further liberation, because this itself is liberation. The means to achieve this end is to follow the classical *ashtanga yoga* (the eight-fold *yoga*). Shankara upholds the *jnana marga* as the ultimate means through which liberation is attained. Remember that he had taught that there is only one thing that is real, and that is Brahman. His theory teaches that our perception of separate things is due to the sway of *maya*. He equates *maya* with ignorance (*avidya*). Therefore the realization of one's true self as Brahman is achieved when ignorance is removed through the path of transcendental knowledge.

Bhakti marga is directed towards the *saguna* Brahman or personal God. Here the renunciation of the world is not directly intended but is the result. God becomes the only object of love for the devotee and attachment to worldly things, as a result, withers away. This path does not demand the suppression of natural impulses but tells the devotee to turn to the Lord[16]. The attainment of *moksha* is not an easy task for simple souls. The devotee surrenders himself to God's will and strives to love the Lord. The divine love is considered the nectar that leads man to immortality. A sincere love for, and devotion to the divine, is regarded as leading the devotee to the Absolute[17]. This path is not limited to the status of any person, but open to all stages, castes, or sexes. Salvation is attainable at any stage of life because it is bestowed upon individuals as an act of divine grace[18]. The love of God makes them closer to God and consequently leads them to communion with Him, which finally releases the souls from *samsara*[19]. Together with the theory of *karma yoga* (the theory of detached actions), the *bhakti* tradition gained rather more prominence[20]. The spiritual life for most of the Hindus today is closely related to the faith in *karma* theory[21]. This means that human actions are binding on the individual soul. Intricately linked is the faith in the transmigration of soul, which means that the soul enters another body after death. The actions of an individual in the previous life determine the status of the present life. The deeds of present life decide the condition of next life. Thus human life is a cycle of births, deaths, and rebirths. Liberation called *moksha,* happens finally when the soul gets out of this cycle or *samsara.* The spiritual pursuit is to save the soul from this cycle. Thus attainment of *moksha* is considered as the supreme goal or aim of spiritual life[22].

In everyday religious world, the high gods are often not the focus[23]. Mostly worship happens at family and the worship is given to the Family gods by the head of the family. The most important deity to a person, the *isht devata* (cherished deity), is a matter of choice. Most Hindus believe that the name of their own god, if recited often, would confer blessings and ultimate redemption[24]. The worship of *isht devata* can be done either at home or in the temple. People who take spiritual life seriously are initiated by a guru and given the name of *isht devata* by the guru as a *mantra* (a word or a couple of words capable of spiritual transformation), which the disciple is supposed to chant at all times.

On the spiritual level, Hinduism is individualistic as it is everyone who has to work for his/her salvation or liberation. The individual soul must bear the fruits of his/her actions. Others have no possibility of helping the salvation of someone else. Although there is the possibility and practice of offering sacrifices and *pujas* in the name of someone else, the liberation is the task of each individual soul. Priesthood is not an organized body, and clerical functions can also be performed by *sadhus, swamis, gurus* etc. The role of intercession and mediation is rather absent in the spirituality. "Worship, on the whole, is done by individuals, not by a collective which can be considered as 'parish'"[25]. The purpose of any of the worship is to awaken the spirit within. For Hindus, the spirituality is all about awakening the spirit, the *atma*, the self, God within[26].

The Rural Hinduism

Unlike the more sophisticated religious practices, specifically the three *margas* of the urban and elite, the practice of religion in the rural context is very different. Village religion has a rather autonomous pattern and is more regulated by social pressures of castes/*varnas* and other practical situations than by any direct indoctrination through religious authorities. Rural religion is mainly concerned with the preservation of life, fertility of man and nature, birth and death, cure from diseases and protection from evil spirits[27]. It is also concerned with the restoration of social harmony and festivals. Every village has its own local god or goddesses and who are often assimilated into the Hindu pantheon through various myths[28].

Faith in the existence of the world of spirits is very strong in the rural Hindu population. They also have faith in the unfavourable constellations of stars and the evil eye. All living beings and even the crops can be affected by these evil spirits, evil eye etc[29]. They believe that the spirit of the departed, especially those who suffered a violent or untimely death, can wander in nature and hurt living beings, especially the relatives. These spirits are considered evil spirits and must be appeased. These evils spirits can possess people, can harm others, and bring disease and disaster to the people and village.

Some wandering spirits are propitiated by offering them a home of worship in the form of a temple or a stone etc. To avoid the evil influence of the demons and ward off the evil spirits, many people wear amulets around the neck or hand[30]. Small children are considered more vulnerable to the sprits, therefore sacred thread of red and black or amulets are tied around their necks, waist, or hand.

There are certain people called *ojhas* who are considered as having supernatural powers and 'evil knowledge' and who can control these spirits. Their help is sought very often in the face of troubles, sickness etc. *Ojhas* are not respected but are rather feared since they are supposed to possess power over evil spirits. Often there is a tendency to believe in truth-tellers, palm readers, astrologists, medical quacks or dream interpreters[31].

Endnotes

[1] Harold Coward, *Sin and Salvation in the World Religions: A Short Introduction,* Oxford, One world, 2007, p.p.90-91.

[2] It is not fatalism, since *karm* can be influenced or even neutralized by religious practices.

[3] *Mokc* (moksha) or liberation is not achieving heaven, but going beyond heaven and hell, beyond happiness and unhappiness.

[4] R.D. Nirakari, 'Rituals and Sacraments in Hinduism: A Historical Perspective', in C.O. McMullen (ed.), *Rituals and Sacraments in Indian Religions,* Delhi, ISPCK, 1979, p. 17.

[5] Attainment of all worldly goodness depended on the grace of gods present in the natural phenomena

[6] R.D. Nirakari, 'Rituals and Sacraments in Hinduism. A Historical Perspective', in C.O. Mcmullen (ed.), *Rituals and Sacraments in Indian Religions,* Delhi, ISPCK, 1979, p. 17.

[7] S. Bhajanananda, 'Hindu Prayer, Worship, Contemplation', in V. MATAJI (ed.), *Shabda Shakti Sangam,* p. 75. Spiritual realization was attainable through the knowledge of oneness with the ultimate.

[8] Nirakari, 'Rituals and Sacraments in Hinduism', p. 18.

[9] Chaitanya Mahaprabhu, Surdas, Vallabha, Kabir, Tulsidas, Tukaram, Ravidas, Namdeo, Meera Bhai and so on were some of the important *bhakti* poets.

[10] Rodrigues, *Introducing Hinduism,* p. 158.

[11] What *karma* one should do is related to the theory of Dharma. One has to perform one's dharma- of the caste and stage of life.

[12] Sharma, *Classical Hindu Thought,* p. 127.

[13] So every caste/*varG* and every stages of life will be preserved.

[14] Bhagavad Gita 2.47.

[15] This is in line with the Vedic utterance like "thou art that" (*tat tvam assi*), "I am Brahman" (*aham brahmasmi*).

[16] Nikhilananda, *Hinduism,* p. 247.

[17] Rodrigues, *Introducing Hinduism,* p. 163.

[18] M.T. Horstmann, 'Bhakti and Monasticism', in G.D. Sontheimer & H. Kulke (eds.), *Hinduism Reconsidered,* Delhi, Manohar Publishers, 1991, p. 127.

[19] M. Das, 'Bhakti Yoga', in V. MatajI (ed.), *Shabda Shakti Sangam*, p. 102.

[20] The theory of *karmayoga* is based on the second chapter verse 47 of Bhagavad Gita which states "Seek to perform your duty but lay not claim on its fruits. Be you not the producer of the fruits of *karma*, neither shall you lean towards inaction." The meaning of the word *karm* is action, while *karmyog* connotes the use of action as a channel of God-realization.

[21] It is not fatalism since *karma* can be influenced or even neutralized by religious practices.

[22] Moksha or liberation is not achieving heaven, but going beyond heaven and hell, beyond happiness and unhappiness.

[23] Michaels, *Hinduism. Past and Present*, p. 215.

[24] Klostermaier, *A Survey of Hinduism*, p. 154.

[25] G. Dietrich, *Culture, Religion and Development*, Bangalore, CSA Publications, 1978, p. 22.

[26] S. Varanath, 'Foundation of the Spiritual life', in V. Mataji (ed.), *Shabda Shakti Sangam*, p. 85.

[27] G. Dietrich, *Culture, Religion and Development*, Bangalore, CSA Publications, 1978, p, p. 59.

[28] Basham, *The Wonder that was India*, p. 319.

[29] A sacred thread is wound around hand or waist to protect the wearer.

[30] Antoine, 'Rituals and Worship', p. 161.

[31] Michaels, *Hinduism. Past and Present*, p. 227.

Chapter - 8

An Introduction to the Christian Presence in Rishikesh

Rishikesh is a confluence of different traditions and religions. Besides the various Hindu traditions, we also have the Sikh Gurudwara, centres for Kabir Panthis, Dadu Panthis, Jain temples and Christian saints and Christian ashrams and centres. Many Christians from west used to visit Sivananda Ashram from the beginning. Although for Swami Sivananda all the religions were equal, in the beginning of the ashram, not all his disciples and devotees had shared this universal attitude. It is said that in the early days of the ashram in 1930s, some

Swami Abhishiktananda

orthodox members of the ashram did not have this welcoming attitude. A Christian friend of Swami Sivananda came to the ashram. Swamiji took him to the dining hall. Seeing the presence of a Christian in their midst, some of the orthodox inmates stopped eating and left the hall. Seeing this Swamiji took the Christian friend to the kitchen itself and made him sit there and he himself served the meals to the Christian friend. This not only stopped the objections, but from then on, the ashram welcomes Christians and members of all religions regularly. Thus from the beginning of the ashram, there were many Christians visiting the ashram and staying there occasionally.

However, the noted first Christian presence in this area in the recent past is in the persons of Abhishiktananda and Sister Therese. Abhishiktananda was born in France on August 30, 1910 and was called Henri Hyacinthe Joseph Marie Le Saux. Although he wanted to come and make India his home immediately after his priestly ordination, he could not come due to several reasons. In 1948 he arrived in South India and joined with Jules Monchanin (1895-1957) a French priest who was living there since 1939. In 1950, together they founded the Shantivanam ashram not far from Trichy and took on the new name Abhishiktananda. He started his Indian life in South India, while frequenting to the Himalayan ranges from 1958. In 1960 he formalized his Indian citizenship and purchased a plot of land at Gyansu near Uttarakashi and built a small hermitage on the banks of the Ganges. This was the hermit-life which he longed and now spent most of his time here. Before this he frequented Rishikesh (from Tamil Nadu) and had a good rapport with Sivananda ashram and in particular with Swami Chidanandaji. Over the twenty-five years between his arrivals in 1948 up to his death in 1973 he lived as an Indian monk.

Interestingly, even before Abhishiktananda, a Greek nun Gerontissa Gavrielia Pappayannis lived for some years in India. She came to India in the year 1955 and worked with Baba Amte and served the poor, especially the leapers. She was called by the inmates of Anandwan (the caring institution for leprosy patients) as sister Leela. After four years of service there she came to the Himalayas and stayed in Uttarakashi for almost one year. Meanwhile she was also associated with Swami Sivananda.

Fr. Yann Vagneux, who has read her personal diary, reports that when she had lived in Uttarakashi, there was no Catholic priest in all these areas. Therefore she prayed to God to send a Catholic priest to this area, and lo, Abhishiktananda who had no idea about her presence or any knowledge of her, came to Uttarakashi a few years later. Returning to Greece, she became a famous spiritual mother. Later in 1963 she returned to India together with another nun sister Tomasina

Therese

and spent three years in Nainital. She also became a friend of Indira Gandhi, the then Prime minister who was cured of her back and shoulder pain by the physiotherapy of mother Gavrielia.

Sr. Therese a French Carmelite from Lisieux came to join Abhishiktananda in India. She arrived in Pondicherry in 1965. In 1967 she came with Abhishiktananda to Haridwar and

Rishikesh and felt a call to remain in this place. In 1971 she spent six months in Haridwar with a Brahmin family. In 1974 she arrived at Sri Vital Ashram, Rishikesh before she moved to Brahmapuri to a kutiya (hut) from where she disappeared in September 1976.

Marc Chaduc was a French disciple of Abhishiktananda who made Rishikesh his home. He was initiated into *Sannyasa* (religious life) in a unique way on 30 June 1973. His initiation into Christian religious life tradition (sannyasa) was led by Abhishiktananda and into the Hindu religious tradition by Chidananda Swami in a single initiation rite made by them exclusively for this purpose. And he received the name Ajatananda (bliss of the non-born). Both the gurus were immensely joyful about their disciple's progress in spiritual life. He was living in a small hermitage just at the banks of Ganges in a place called Kaudiyala on the Rishikesh Srinagar road. However, he disappeared in April 1977. We have no further information about his later life as no one has seen him in the later part of his life.

Swami Ajatananda

Jeevandhara *Sadhana* Kutir

Jeevandhara *Sadhana* Kutir, at the banks of River Ganges at Tapovan, Rishikesh was founded by Vandana Mataji and by Ishapriya (Sister Patricia Kinsey) of the Society of the Sacred Heart in the year 1978. Vandana Mataji as she came to be called had also started the Jeevandhara Ashram at Jaiharikhal where she guided it for 12 years before returning to Tapovan. Earlier she had stayed at the Divine Life Society in Rishikesh, studying and practicing the Indian *sannyasa* from Swami Chidananda. By her association with several spiritual masters of India, through her commitment to a life of Indian *sannyasa* and by living in several Christian and Hindu ashrams she discovered a true Indian Christian face. First of all she transformed herself into an authentically 'Indian face' of the Christian faith.[1] Vandana Mataji purchased a small plot of land at the banks of Ganges to continue her spiritual pilgrimage. Many people especially from western background sought after her guidance. At present Turiya Mataji runs this ashram where she gives opportunity for retreats, meditations and *satsanghs*.

Prithvipal Sadan

Prithvipal Sadan, situated in Tapovan is a Catholic Church of the ancient St. Thomas Christians of India. They are also called Syrian Christians, who trace their origin to Thomas, one of the 12 disciples of Jesus who came to India in the first century (in 52 AD) and established Christianity in the Malabar cost (Kerala). Although this Christianity in India is as old as Christianity itself, it did not spread outside the Malabar cost. Both the western Christians and the North Indian Hindus did not have much knowledge and contact with these Christians.

Although several individual members of this community had spread to all parts of the world, they had not established churches as such outside Kerala. Pritvipal Sadan was started in the year 1980. This Church of the indigenous Christians stands as a witness to the religious harmony and basic oneness of the religious traditions. Sunday Eucharist is conducted mostly in Hindi and the tradition followed is the ancient Syro-Malabar rite. The very shape of the church and its architecture, the artwork inside the church and the entrance etc., all present an Indian face of Christianity.

Aranya Ashram

Aranya is a small ashram near Ganges at Tapovan, which follows a way of life focused on contemplation and inter-spirituality. The Sanskrit word "Aranya" means "forest or desert" and stands as a symbol of mystical union with the Divine and serious spiritual effort.

Aranya Ashram is inspired by the tradition of the Hermits of Saccidananda in the Shantivanam Ashram founded by Jules Monchanin and Abhishiktananda. Hospitality is the main form of service, especially offered to spiritual seekers and the local women and children. The foundress and co-ordinator of this ashram is Australian origin Carrie Lock, locally known as "Aranya" (after the ashram).

At Aranya Ashram, the approach and teachings are inter-spiritual: drawing on the mystical wisdom of the various spiritual traditions, whilst at the same time being practical and down-to-earth - appreciating the whole person: body, mind and soul. "Your story matters", says Aranya. Mataji Aranya at the ashram offers spiritual talks, prayer and meditation sessions, individual spiritual guidance, residential retreats (for women), and one day retreats for men and women. Presently Mataji prefers to spend more time in silence and solitude and not much keen on giving sessions unless necessary.

Ajatananda Ashram

It is an inter-religious monastic ashram named after Swami Ajatananda Saraswati (Marc Chaduc) a disciple of Swami Abhishiktananda. This ashram situated on the banks of River Ganges at Tapovan operates as a monastic (sannyasa) ashram. Ajatananda Ashram is an experiment and an attempt to live one's interiority with one another as a form of dialogue. The community at ashram does not involve rituals of any kind, except for short prayers and some chanting in the evening, and some short spiritual readings in the morning. No common worship is held in the Ashram. The present head Swami Atmananda Udasin who has discarded his Christian identity and accepted Hinduism offers regular *satsanghs* in the evening from 16.00 to 17.30 hours except Thursdays.

Samanvaya Vidya Dham

Samanvaya Vidya Dham at Tapovan is a Catholic ashram mainly for the Scholastics of the CMI Religious Congregation. Before moving into the present site, they stayed at Prithvipal Sadan which is the Catholic Church of the diocese of Bijnor from 1995 to 2008. The aim of this Vidya Dham is primarily for their scholastics to be immersed in the inter-religious context of Rishikesh which would help them to imbibe the spirit of Indian religiosity and spirituality actively present here. They practice the Christian *Sadhana*, in the Hindu spiritual context, devoting themselves to deep and intense study of theology and scriptures as well as engaging in meditation, yoga and *satsanghs*, with openness to the other religious traditions and gurus.

The students of Samanvaya come to Rishikesh as part of their fourteen and a half years of formation and training to religious life and Priesthood. After having completed 12 years, and after the first-year of theological formation in the tribal-subaltern context of Bastar (Chattisgarh), they come to the interreligious context of Rishikesh. Here the students take a serious theological reflection in the context of great sages and saints, pilgrims and seekers who are engaged in various kinds of spiritual *sadhana*. The students are given ample opportunity to be open to the followers of other religions while discovering the person and mission of Jesus.

Jesus the Amar Guru at Samanvaya Chapel

They are led to discover Jesus as the human face of the divine compassion in their manifold encounters with the hermits, seekers and *sannyasis* of Rishikesh. As Raimon Panikkar said, "In a multi-religious country like India, to be a religious person is to be an inter-religious person". It is not a tolerance but rather it is transforming and enriching of oneself as a better human person through dialogue with other faith-holders. Since everyone has origin in God and the entire human race is like a large family the inter-religious context of Rishikesh helps the theological search to become more inclusive.

Endnotes

[1] L. Malieckal, "Vandana Mataji: An Icon of the Indian Face of Christian Faith" in *Jesus the Human Face of God*, ed., Cyril Kuttiyanikkal, Delhi: ISPCK, 2019,p. 283.

Bibliography

Abhishiktananda, *Guru and Disciple,* London, ISPCK, 1974.

-------, *Saccidananda. A Christian Approach to Advaitic Experience,* Delhi, ISPCK, 1974.

Asharose, 'Shiva', in V. Mataji (ed.), *Shabda Shakti Sangam,* Rishikesh, Jeevan-dhara *Sadhana* Kutir, 1995.

Ashirvatham, E., *Christianity in the Indian Crucible,* Calcutta, YMCA Publishing House, 1957.

Basham, A.L., *The Wonder that was India,* London, Sidwick & Jackson, 1968.

Bhajanananda, S., 'Hinyer, Worship, Contemplation',in', in V. Mataji (ed.), *Shabda Shakti Sangam,* Rishikesh, Jeevan Dhara *Sadhana* Kutir,1995.

Bhojraj, Dwivedi., *Religious Basics of Hindu Beliefs,* New Delhi, Diamond Books, 2010.

Castellino, J., *Becoming an Indian Guru-Priest,* Shillong, Vendrame Missiological Institute, 1982.

Cave, S., *Redemption. Hindu and Christian,* London, Oxford University Press, 1919.

Chatterjee, Gautam., *Sacred Hindu Symbols,* Delhi, Abhinav Publications, 2003.

Chenchiah, P., 'The Church and the Indian Christian', in D.M. Devasahayam & A.N. Sudarisanam (eds.), *Rethinking Christianity in India,* Madras, A.N. Sudarisanam, 1935.

Collins, P.M., *Context, Culture and Worship. The Quest for Indian-ness*, Delhi, ISPCK, 2006.

Coward, Harold, *Sin and Salvation in the World Religions: A Short Introduction*, Oxford, One world, 2007.

Das, M., 'Bhakti Yoga', in V. MatajI (ed.), *Shabda Shakti Sangam*, Rishikesh, Jeevan Dhara *Sadhana* Kutir,1995.

Deussen, Paul., *Sixty Upanishads of the Veda*, Delhi, Motilal Banarsidass, 1997.

Dietrich, G., *Culture, Religion and Development*, Bangalore, CSA Publications, 1978.

Ezhaparampil, Manuel., *Formation to Discipleship*, Bangalore, Claretian Publications, 2004.

Fallon, P., 'The Gods of Hinduism', in R. Antoine, et al, (eds.), *Religious Hinduism. A Presentation and Appraisal*, Allahabad, St. Paul Publications, 1968.

Flood, Gavin. *An Introduction to Hinduism*. New Delhi: Foundation Books, 2004.

Ghurye, G.S., *Indian Sadhus*, Bombay, The Popular Book Depot, 1953.

Giri, S.N., 'The Guru in Hindu Tradition', in V. Mataji (ed.), *Christian Ashrams*.

Gross, Robert Lewis, *The Sadhus of India: A Study of Hindu Asceticism*, New Delhi/Jaipur, Rawat Publications,1992.

Horstmann, M.T., 'Bhakti and Monasticism', in G.D. Sontheimer & H. Kulke (eds.), *Hinduism Reconsidered*, Delhi, Manohar Publishers, 1991.

Karokaran, A., *Evangelization and Diakonia*, Bangalore, Dharmaram ications, 1978.

Klostermaier, K.K., A *Survey of Hinduism*, New York, State University of New York Press, 1989.

Kuttiyanikkal C.J., *Khrist Bhakta Movement: A Model for an Indian Church?*, Munster/London, LiT Verlag, 2014.

Malieckal, Louis., 'Vandana Mataji: An Icon of the Indian Face of Christian Faith' in Cyril Kuttiyanikkal ed., *Jesus the Human Face of God*, Delhi, ISPCK, 2019.

Mataji, V., *Gurus, Ashrams and Christians*, Madras, The Christian Literature Society, 1980.

------, V., 'Finding Our Roots before We Take Wing', in V. Mataji (ed.), *Christian Ashrams. A Movement with a Future?* Delhi, ISPCK, 1993.

Menen, Aubrey, *The Mystics*, New York, The Dial Press, 1974.

Michaels, A., *Hinduism. Past and Present*, trans. Barbara Harshav, Princeton University Press, 1998.

Nikhilananda, S., *Hinduism. Its Meaning for the Liberation of the Spirit*, London, George Allen & Unwin Ltd, 1958.

Nirakari, R.D., 'Rituals and Sacraments in Hinduism. A Historical Perspective', in C.O. Mcmullen (ed.), *Rituals and Sacraments in Indian Religions*, Delhi, ISPCK, 1979.

Nityesthananda, S., 'The Concept of God in Hinduism', in V. Mataji (ed.), *Shabda Shakti Sangam*, Rishikesvan Dhara *Sadhana* Kutir,1995.

Olivelle, P., *The Asrama System. The History and Hermeneutics of a Religious Institution*, New York/Oxford, Oxford University Press, 1993.

Painadath, S., (ed.), *Solitude and Solidarity*, Aikya/ISPCK, 2003.

Palispis, E.S., *Introduction to Values Education*, Quezon City, Rex Book Store, 1995.

Ralston, Ho, *Christian Ashrams. A New Religious Movement in Contemporary India*, Lewiston/Queenston, The Edwin Mellen Press, 1987.

Rodrigues, H., *Introducing Hinduism*, New York/London, Routledge, 2006.

Schouten, J.P., *Jesus as Guru. The Image of Christ among Hindus and Christians in India*, Amsterdam/ New York, Rodopi, 2008.

Sharma, A., *Classical Hindu Thought. An Introduction*, Oxford, Oxford University Press, 2000.

Sharma, B.N.K., *Philosophy of Sri Madhavcarya*, Delhi, Motilal Banarsidas, 1986.

Sivananda, Sri Swami., *Meditation on Om and Mandukya Upanishad*, Shivanandanagar, The Divine Life Society, 1985.

Smith, D., *Hinduism and Modernity*, Malden, Blackwell publishing, 2003.

Taylor, R.W., *Acknowledging the Lordship of Christ*, Delhi, ISPCK, 1992.

Thottakara, A., *Indian Spirituality,* Bangalore, Dharmaram Publications, 2005, p.45

Tilak, Shrinavas, *Religion and Aging in Indian Tradition,* New York, State University of New York Press, 1989.

Tola, Fernando & Carmen Dragonetti, *The Yogasutras of Patanjali: On Concentration of mind,* translated by K. D. Prithipaul, Delhi, Motilal Banarsidas Publishers, 1987.

Tyagimai, 'The Role of the Guru and the *Ashram* in the Hindu Tradition', in V. Mataji (ed.), *Shabda Shakti Sangan,* Rishikesh, Jeevan Dhara *Sadhana* Kutir,1995.

Underhill, M.M., *The Hindu Religious Year,* New Delhi, Asian Educations Services, 2001.

Varanath, S., 'Foundation of the Spiritual life', in V. Mataji (ed.), *Shabda Shakti Sangam,* Rishikesh, Jeevan Dhara Sadhana Kutir,1995.

Vandana, *Gurus, Ashrams and Christians,* Bombay, St. Paul Publications, 1978.

Weber, M., *The Religion of India,* Illinois, The Free Press, 1960.

Wilfred, F., *Beyond Settled Foundations. The Journey of Indian Theology,* Madras, Department of Christian Studies University of Madras, 1999.

Wilkins, W.J., *Modern Hinduism,* New Delhi, Cosmo Publications, 1985.

Index

9 789390 569007